Journal of the Shenandoah Valley During the Civil War Era

Volume III
2020

Jonathan A. Noyalas
Editor

A publication of Shenandoah University's McCormick Civil War Institute

Copyright © 2020 Shenandoah University's McCormick Civil War Institute
All rights reserved.

ISSN: 2639-6815
ISBN: 978-1797719986

Editorial Advisory Board

Jonathan M. Berkey	Concord University
Ryan Bixby	Three Rivers College
James J. Broomall	Shepherd University
Eric A. Campbell	Cedar Creek & Belle Grove National Historical Park
Dennis E. Frye	Harpers Ferry National Historical Park
Keith E. Gibson	Virginia Military Institute
Allen C. Guelzo	Princeton University
Terence M. Heder	Shenandoah Valley Battlefields Foundation
John J. Hennessy	National Park Service
Brian Matthew Jordan	Sam Houston State University
Barton A. Myers	Washington & Lee University
Kenneth W. Noe	Auburn University
Kevin R. Pawlak	Ben Lamond Historic Site
Jonathan Steplyk	Texas Christian University
Nancy T. Sorrells	Independent Historian

Copy Editor

Elizabeth Guiliano	Professor Emeritus Lord Fairfax Community College

Manuscript Submissions and Books for Review

The *Journal of the Shenandoah Valley During the Civil War* is published annually by Shenandoah University's McCormick Civil War Institute. Manuscript submissions can be sent to the editor at jnoyalas01@su.edu. Manuscripts should not exceed 10,000 words in length (including footnotes). Books for review consideration can be sent to the editor at the *Journal of the Shenandoah Valley During the Civil War's* editorial home: Jonathan A. Noyalas, director McCormick Civil War Institute, Davis Hall 115, 1460 University Drive, Winchester, VA 22601.

Cover image, "Maryland Heights: Siege of Harper's Ferry" by William MacLeod (Open access image courtesy of National Gallery of Art, Washington, D.C., Corcoran Collection, Gift of Genevieve Plummer, 2016.22.12)

Any opinions expressed in this publication are solely those of the contributing author and do not necessarily reflect the viewpoints of the editor, editorial advisory board, Shenandoah University, or the McCormick Civil War Institute.

Contents

From the Editor

Reflecting on Mark Twain's "Memory-Builder"
    Jonathan A. Noyalas..1

Feature Essays

"The Shenandoah Chanting Its Endless Requiem": A Roster of Cool Spring's Union Dead
    Jake Gabriele, Victor Hererra, Jonathan A. Noyalas, Sarah Powell & Shelby R. Shrader..3

"Battery G Soon Made it Uncomfortable for the Rebels that They Ceased Firing": Battery G, First Rhode Island Light Artillery and the Opening of the 1864 Valley Campaign
    Robert Grandchamp..30

"In Order that He May Have the Opportunity to Attend School and Fit Himself for the Duties of a Free Man": Reforming Black Minors' Labor in the Post-Emancipation Shenandoah Valley
    Donna Dodenhoff..45

"Hardships and Dangers Will Bind Men as Brothers": The 170th Ohio National Guard in the Summer of 1864
    Jon-Erik Gilot..65

"Uncle John Bowman's and his Uncle Sam and Their Families are Going to Ohio": Sheridan's Refugee Wagon Train
    Prue Engle Yelinek..84

Judge Richard Parker's Loyalty: The Parker-Imboden Correspondence, Spring 1864
    Trish Ridgeway...107

Book Reviews..123

Notes on Contributors..147

From the Editor

Reflecting on Mark Twain's "Memory-Builder"

Jonathan A. Noyalas

As Mark Twain put the finishing touches on *Huckleberry Finn* in his study at his home in Hartford, Connecticut, in the mid-1880s, he grappled with developing a method to aid his daughters in understanding history. Always innovative, Twain created a game, "Mark Twain's Memory-Builder." As Twain constructed the game and crafted language to go with it he contemplated history's events and how individuals should weigh history's grand moments against those regarded as less significant. After deliberation, Twain concluded that although aspects of history people might consider minor are not as "showy and picturesque" as compared to significant ones, they are nonetheless "valuable" and important to a broader understanding of history's complexities.[1]

Much of this volume elucidates events and people some might consider minor but are essential to understanding the Civil War era's complexities in the Shenandoah Valley.

Volume 3 of *Journal of the Shenandoah Valley During the Civil War Era* contains three essays in some way connected to the Battle of Cool Spring. These essays have particular relevance to the McCormick Civil War Institute's work at the 195 acres of the battlefield under the care of Shenandoah University. One of these essays showcases nearly two years of research conducted by some of the best and brightest students I have had the great fortune to teach and mentor at Shenandoah University. Although this volume marks the first time undergraduate students in Civil War studies

---

[1] Mark Twain's Memory-Builder, accessed August 21, 2019, http://twain.lib.virginia.edu/marketin/memory.html

have contributed to the *Journal*, I do not anticipate it being the last. I am also hopeful, as is the entire editorial board, that colleagues at other colleges and universities will encourage advanced undergraduate and graduate students who might be researching a topic related to the Shenandoah Valley's Civil War era history to consider submitting an essay.

In addition to the essays connected to Cool Spring, volume 3 contains contributions examining apprenticeships for African Americans in the Civil War's immediate aftermath, issues of Judge Richard Parker's loyalty, and the wagon train of refugees from Rockingham County in the autumn of 1864. Our book review section rounds out this volume highlighting books directly related to the Shenandoah Valley's Civil War era story or ones that can in some way provide historical context and offer a framework for better understanding various aspects of the Valley's Civil War era history.

"The Shenandoah Chanting its Endless Requiem"
A Roster of Cool Spring's Union Dead

Jake Gabriele, Victor Herrera, Jonathan A. Noyalas, Sarah Powell & Shelby R. Shrader

Among the fifteen major battles fought in the Shenandoah Valley, the Battle of Cool Spring is arguably the least recognizable.[2] The battles of Confederate general Thomas J. "Stonewall" Jackson's 1862 Valley Campaign and Union general Philip H. Sheridan's 1864 Shenandoah Campaign are well-known and have received much attention from scholars. The Battle of New Market, statistically smaller than Cool Spring, has received wide-attention, its popularity stemming in part from the role cadets from the Virginia Military Institute played at the battle. Although not as familiar as Jackson's victory at Port Republic or Sheridan's smashing success at Cedar Creek, to the Union and Confederate soldiers who fought and sacrificed at Cool Spring and to the families of those who had husbands, sons, and brothers killed in the battle, the fighting along the banks of the Shenandoah on July 18, 1864, proved the war's most significant moment.

---

[2] While 326 different military actions occurred in the Shenandoah Valley, the fifteen major battles considered here are: the First Battle of Kernstown (March 23, 1862); Battle of McDowell (May 8, 1862); Battle of Front Royal (May 23, 1862); the First Battle of Winchester (May 25, 1862); Battle of Cross Keys (June 8, 1862); Battle of Port Republic (June 9, 1862); Second Battle of Winchester (June 13-15, 1863); Battle of New Market (May 15, 1864); Battle of Piedmont (June 5, 1864); Battle of Cool Spring (July 18, 1864); Second Battle of Kernstown (July 24, 1864); Third Battle of Winchester (September 19, 1864); Battle of Fisher's Hill (September 22, 1864); Battle of Tom's Brook (October 9, 1864); and the Battle of Cedar Creek (October 19, 1864). Heritage Partners, Inc. and John Milner Associates, Inc., *Shenandoah Valley Battlefields National Historic District: Final Management Plan* (New Market, VA: Shenandoah Valley Battlefields National Historic District, 2000), i. Some lists might include additional engagements such as Battle of Rutherford's Farm (July 20, 1864) and Battle of Waynesboro (March 2, 1865).

Since Shenandoah University acquired 195 acres of the Cool Spring Battlefield in 2013, Shenandoah University's McCormick Civil War Institute assumed the awesome and important responsibility of all interpretive and educational efforts at Cool Spring. Amidst the time-consuming work of developing tours, designing exhibitions, conducting special programs, and installing interpretive signs, the McCormick Civil War Institute, since the summer of 2018, has been identifying and researching the backgrounds of the Union and Confederate soldiers killed at Cool Spring or those who died as a result of wounds received at the battle. This roster of Union dead is the first step in resurrecting individual stories of sacrifice, heroism, and tragedy at Cool Spring. Work continues on researching Cool Spring's Confederate dead. That roster will be published in volume 4 of *Journal of the Shenandoah Valley During the Civil War Era*.

This roster, first and foremost, reveals some important demographic information about federal troops who perished at Cool Spring. Among the seventy-two Union soldiers either killed at the battle or who died days after as a result of wounds received, the average age was twenty-seven. The youngest soldier, Private Washington Hiatt of the 15th West Virginia, was sixteen. At fifty-two-years-old Peter Hersch, 54th Pennsylvania, was the oldest. An examination of compiled service records, widows' pensions, casualty reports, and regimental rosters illuminates the types of injuries Union soldiers received at Cool Spring. Although most records do not specifically note the type of wound, some do. Of the thirteen Union soldiers on this roster whose records indicate the precise cause of death, seven were shot in the head, five drowned in the Shenandoah River during the Union retreat, and one was shot in the heart. Seven of the soldiers included on this roster received mortal wounds and died days after the battle.

In addition to providing a demographic snapshot, this roster of Union dead offers a powerful reminder of war's tragic consequences. Nineteen of the soldiers on this roster were married and had children. Cool Spring then not only cut short the lives of individuals, but made wives into widows and left children fatherless.

This roster serves not only as an enumeration to aid individuals who study and visit Cool Spring understand the battle's statistical toll, but more significantly to contemplate the impact it had on human beings—soldiers and the ones they left behind.

1st West Virginia Infantry

Joshua B. Lukens (Private)

Joshua B. Lukens was born January 12, 1845, in Wheeling, Virginia (West Virginia). At the age of eighteen Lukens enlisted in the 1st Virginia Infantry (U.S.) on September 24, 1861. Lukens' enlistment record noted that he had a light complexion, grey eyes, and was 5' 9" tall. He was killed at Cool Spring. Private Lukens is buried in Greenwood Cemetery, Wheeling, West Virginia.[3]

2nd Maryland Eastern Shore Infantry

Edward Bausley (private)

On August 30, 1862, Bausley enlisted in the 2nd Maryland Eastern Shore. He was killed slightly more than two years later at Cool Spring.[4] Bausley is buried in the Winchester National Cemetery, grave 3998.

Peter Chalron (private)

Peter Chalron was born in Canada in 1835. He moved from Canada to Baltimore, Maryland, at an unknown time and found work as a shoemaker in the city. He enlisted in the 2nd Maryland Eastern Shore Infantry in Baltimore on February 8, 1864. According to his enlistment papers, Chalron was, "29 years old, 5 feet 4 inches high, had blue eyes, light hair, and a light complexion." While defending the Union right flank against Confederate general Robert Rodes' flank attack at Cool Spring, Chalron was "killed by reason of being shot through the head by a musket ball." Because of the Union retreat, Chalron's body was unable to be taken to the east

---

[3] Joshua B. Lukens, 1st West Virginia Infantry, Compiled Service Record, National Archives and Records Administration, Washington D.C. (additional references to Compiled Service Records at the National Archives will be noted as CSR, NARA); Joshua B. Lukens, Mother's Pension Records, Case Files of Approved Pension Applications of Widows and Other Veterans of the Army and Navy Who Served Mainly in the Civil War and War with Spain, Compiled 1861-1934, National Archives and Records Administration, Washington D.C. (additional references to Mothers Pension Records at the National Archives will be noted as MPR, NARA).
[4] L. Allison Wilmer, J.H. Jarrett, George W.F. Vernon, *History and Roster of Maryland Volunteers, War of 1861-5* (Baltimore, MD: Press of Guggenheimer, Weil, & Co., 1898), 1: 632.

bank of the river during the battle. Upon returning to retrieve the bodies after the battle, Chalron's comrades noted that his personal effects were gone. On his casualty sheet, Captain William Jones noted, "The regiment was compelled to retake the effects that were in the hands of the enemy." Chalron's body is buried in the Winchester National Cemetery, grave 4007.[5]

4th West Virginia Infantry

Francis Clendenin (sergeant)

Francis Clendenin was born in Mason City, Virginia, (West Virginia) in 1845. He enlisted in the 4th West Virginia Infantry on September 18, 1861. He mustered into the regiment on September 27, 1861. He was promoted to corporal in Company I on October 7, 1862. He continued to rise through the ranks, being "Promoted to Sergeant for bravery in action, May 19, 1863." After Clendenin's enlistment expired on January 20, 1864, he reenlisted in the regiment as a veteran volunteer. Half-a-year after his reenlistment Clendenin was killed at Cool Spring. The location of his remains is unknown.[6]

Walter Gard (corporal)

Twenty-two-year-old Walter Gard enlisted in the 4th West Virginia Infantry on July 21, 1861. By the time of his death at Cool Spring he held the rank of corporal. At first buried on the battlefield, Gard was later interred in grave 3887 in Winchester National Cemetery.[7]

John Hinsix (private)

He enlisted in the 4th West Virginia Infantry and was mustered into Company B. He was killed in action at Cool Spring. The location of Private Hinsix's remains is unknown.[8]

---

[5] Peter Chalron, 2nd Maryland Eastern Shore Infantry, CSR, NARA.
[6] Francis Clendenin, 4th West Virginia Infantry, CSR, NARA.
[7] "Military Monday—Resurrecting Cpl. Walter Gard," accessed June 28, 2019, http://kithandkinchronicles.blogspot.com/2015/03/military-monday-resurrecting-cpl-walter.html
[8] John Hinsix, 4th West Virginia Infantry, CSR, NARA; John Hinsix, 4th West Virginia Infantry, MPR, NARA.

George W. Houson (corporal)

A potter from Ohio, George W. Houson enlisted in Company D, 4th West Virginia Infantry on July 8, 1861. When his three-year enlistment expired Houson reenlisted in the 4th West Virginia as a veteran volunteer. At the time of his reenlistment on January 21, 1864, Houson was promoted to the rank of corporal. He was killed in action at Cool Spring.[9]

John Kinser (private)

On July 5, 1861, Kinser enlisted in the regiment. On January 1, 1864, he reenlisted in the 4th as a veteran volunteer. He was killed at the Battle of Cool Spring. Kinser is buried in the Winchester National Cemetery, grave 3696.[10]

Isaac Kitterman (private)

Isaac N. Kitterman was born in Jackson County, Virginia (West Virginia), in 1839. He worked as a laborer prior to the conflict. On July 25, 1861, Kitterman crossed the Ohio River and entered the town of Gallipolis in order to enlist in the 4th. He was mustered in as a private on August 11. On April 10, 1863, while on campaign in Louisiana, Kitterman was admitted to the hospital in Millikens Bend due to sickness. He was then transferred to a hospital in St. Louis, Missouri, later that month, before returning to the regiment in September 1863. After his enlistment expired on January 19, 1864, Kitterman reenlisted as a veteran volunteer. He was killed in action at the battle and buried in the Winchester National Cemetery, grave 3914.[11]

Moses Knapp (private)

Moses Knapp was born in either 1844 or 1845. He enlisted in the 4th on July 25, 1861, and was mustered in to Company G on August 11, 1861. Records indicate that he constantly battled illness throughout his service. He met his fate at Cool Spring at the age of twenty-two.[12]

---

[9] George W. Houson, 4th West Virginia Infantry, CSR, NARA.
[10] *Annual Report of the Adjutant General of the State of West Virginia for the Year Ending December 31, 1864* (Wheeling, WV: John F. M'Dermot, Public Printer, 1865), 80.
[11] Isaac Kitterman, 4th West Virginia Infantry, CSR, NARA.
[12] Moses Knapp, 4th West Virginia Infantry, CSR, NARA.

George A. Scott (first lieutenant)

George A. Scott enlisted in the regiment at the age of eighteen. He mustered into Company F as a corporal. He was promoted to first sergeant in early 1862. On January 4, 1863, he was promoted to second lieutenant. He rose to the rank of first lieutenant on May 22, 1863—the rank he held at the time of Cool Spring. His compiled service record offers conflicting accounts of his fate at Cool Spring. Portions of his record indicate that he was wounded at the battle and sent home on furlough to recuperate from his wounds. Other documents in Scott's file state he was killed outright at Cool Spring, an unlikely scenario considering his file includes reports indicating his being examined by a doctor in the weeks after the battle and later succumbing to the wounds he received at Cool Spring.[13]

5th New York Heavy Artillery

William E. Barrett (private)

William E. Barrett was born in Utica, New York. Prior to war he worked as a clerk. He enlisted in the 23rd New York on May 16, 1861, at the age of twenty-one for a period of two years. On March 24, 1862, he enlisted into Company C, 5th New York Heavy Artillery. Barrett was killed at Cool Spring and buried in Rome Cemetery, Oneida, New York.[14]

Jonathan G. Berry (private)

Twenty-five-year-old Jonathan Berry mustered into the 5th New York Heavy Artillery as a sergeant in January 1862, and he was killed at Cool Spring. The location of his remains is unknown.[15]

Joseph Boylan (private)

Joseph Boylan was born in Ireland in 1829, where he worked as a laborer before coming to the United States. Having settled in

---

[13] George A. Scott, 4th West Virginia, CSR, NARA; George A. Scott, 4th West Virginia Infantry, MPR, NARA.
[14] William E. Barrett, 5th New York Heavy Artillery, CSR, NARA; William E. Barrett, 5th New York Heavy Artillery, MPR, NARA.
[15] *Annual Report of the Adjutant-General of the State of New York for the Year 1896: Registers of the Fifth and Sixth Artillery in the War of the Rebellion* (Albany, NY: Wynkoop Hallenbeck Crawford Co., 1897), 36.

New York City, he enlisted in Company A, 5th New York Heavy Artillery on November 25, 1863. He perished at Cool Spring. The location of his remains is unknown.[16]

James Burns (private)

Thirty-eight-year-old James Burns mustered into the 5th New York Heavy Artillery in January 1864. Burns had two children, William, who was born in 1858 and Susan, who was born in 1859. Slightly less than one year after Burns' death at Cool Spring, his wife, Margaret, abandoned the children. She left them under the guardianship of James Reiley, who served in the 16th New York.[17]

Charles Busch (private)

Brooklyn-native Charles Busch mustered into Company A, 5th New York Heavy Artillery on December 7, 1863. Busch was killed in action at Cool Spring. The location of his remains is unknown.[18]

Charles Hugh Campbell (private)

Charles Hugh Campbell was born in Boston, Massachusetts. On March 12, 1864, at the age of twenty-seven, he mustered into the 5th New York Heavy Artillery. Before enlisting he worked as a laborer. The description in his service record states Campbell had hazel eyes, brown hair, and was five feet, eight inches in height. Campbell was killed at Cool Spring and the whereabouts of his remains are unknown.[19]

Hugh Carlisle (private)

Hugh Carlisle was born in 1841 in New York and worked as a machinist prior to his enlistment in the 5th New York Heavy Artillery on February 10, 1862. On March 6, 1863, Carlisle was promoted to corporal. He was killed at Cool Spring. Reports indicate that he was

---

[16] Joseph Boylan Abstract Muster Roll, New York Civil War Muster Roll Abstracts, 1861-1900, New York State Archives, Albany, NY.
[17] James Burns, 5th New York Heavy Artillery, CSR, NARA; James Burns, 5th New York Heavy Artillery, MPR, NARA.
[18] *Annual Report of the Adjutant General of the State of New York*, 78.
[19] Charles Hugh Campbell, 5th New York Heavy Artillery, CSR, NARA; Charles Hugh Campbell, 5th New York Heavy Artillery, MPR, NARA.

initially buried at W. H. Belmer's Farm but later interred in the Winchester National Cemetery, grave 922.[20]

Edward Chevalier (private)

Twenty-eight at the time of his enlistment in January 1864, Edward Chevalier was mortally wounded at the Battle of Cool Spring. He was sent to a U.S. hospital in Sandy Hook, Maryland. He died from wounds received at Cool Spring on July 31, 1864.[21]

James Darrah (private)

James Darrah was born in 1834 in Manchester, England, to Daniel and Mary Darrah. His family moved to Massachusetts, and eventually settled in the town of Holyoke. James then began working as a manufacturer in a factory in Springfield. In 1857, James married Amy Carter, a resident of West Springfield, Massachusetts. She was born in Canada in 1837, and migrated to Springfield with her parents, John and Charlotte Carter. On June 16, 1857, James and Amy were married in Holyoke. The couple had one daughter, Minnie, born on March 22, 1861. Darrah mustered into Company C, 5th New York Heavy Artillery in December 1863 in Brooklyn, New York.[22] After his death at Cool Spring one of his regimental comrades, J. A. Blackmon, penned a letter to Darrah's wife: "Mrs. Darrah, I have sad news to communicate. Your husband, James Darrah... was shot through the head at the Battle of Snicker's Gap, July 18th and killed instantly. 3 or 4 members of the company informed that they knew positively that he was killed in the manner above mentioned, and that they saw the place where he was buried" on the battlefield.[23]

John F. Davis (corporal)

John F. Davis, a farmer, was born in Williamstown, Massachusetts. He was twenty-four-years-old at the time he mustered into the regiment in September 1862. On January 22, 1862,

---

[20] Hugh Carlisle, 5th New York Heavy Artillery, CSR, NARA; Hugh Carlisle, 5th New York Heavy Artillery, MPR, NARA.
[21] *Annual Report of the Adjutant General of the State of New York*, 101.
[22] James Darrah Abstract Muster Roll, New York Civil War Muster Roll Abstracts, 1861-1900, New York State Archives, Albany, New York.
[23] James Darrah, 5th New York Heavy Artillery, Widows Pension, National Archives and Records Administration, Washington, D.C. (Items from Widows Pension hereafter cited as WP, NARA).

he was promoted to corporal, the rank he held at the time of his death at Cool Spring.[24]

Darius Ellis (private)

Darius S. Ellis was born May 27, 1843. At the age of eighteen he mustered into the 5th in Cortland, New York. Severely wounded at the battle, Ellis was sent to a hospital in Annapolis, Maryland. He died on October 18, 1864 in Annapolis, as a result of complications from the wound he received at Cool Spring. Ellis is buried in Hartford Mills Cemetery in Hartford Mills, Cortland County, New York.[25]

Christopher Kenner (private)

Christopher Kenner was born in Germany in 1845. He came to the United States, settled in New York, and found work as a shoemaker in Brooklyn. According to his enlistment record, Kenner was "5 feet 5 inches high, with grey eyes, sandy hair, and a light complexion." The form noted that he was "also borne as Christofer, Christoff, and Christof," making recordkeeping somewhat difficult.[26] Kenner enlisted in the 5th New York Heavy Artillery on June 4, 1862, at the age of nineteen. He was promoted to corporal on October 6, 1863. He held that rank at the time of his death at Cool Spring.[27]

Augustus Lampman (private)

Twenty-three-year-old Augustus Lampman enlisted in the 5th New York Heavy Artillery on January 2, 1864. Lampman was wounded at the battle and succumbed to his wounds ten days later. Private Lampman was buried in Butler-Savannah Cemetery in Savannah, Wayne County, New York.[28]

---

[24] John F. Davis, 5th New York Heavy Artillery, CSR, NARA; John F. Davis, 5th New York Heavy Artillery, MPR, NARA.
[25] Darius Ellis, 5th New York Heavy Artillery, CSR, NARA; Darius Ellis, 5th New York Heavy Artillery, MPR, NARA.
[26] Christopher Kenner Abstract Muster Roll, New York Civil War Muster Roll Abstracts, 1861-1900, New York State Archives, Albany, New York.
[27] *Annual Report of the Adjutant General of the State of New York*, 327.
[28] Augustus Lampman, 5th New York Heavy Artillery, CSR, NARA; Augustus Lampman, 5th New York Heavy Artillery, MPR, NARA.

Thomas Lantry (private)

Thomas Lantry was born in 1821. He mustered into the regiment on March 31, 1864. After his death at Cool Spring, his wife Catherine, whom he married in Newark, New Jersey, in 1839, filed for a widow's pension. She received $8 per month and $2 additional for their children, Francis and William Henry.[29]

Private Charles H. Mallory (private)

Charles H. Mallory was born in 1844 in Ohio. He worked as a farmer prior to the war. In March 1864, at the age of twenty, he mustered into the 5th New York Heavy Artillery at Dix, New York. He perished four months later at Cool Spring.[30]

Alexander McClure (sergeant)

Alexander McClure mustered into the 5th New York Heavy Artillery in February 1862. During the regiment's retreat across the Shenandoah River he was reported as being separated from the unit and killed. McClure's wife, Eliza, whom he married on September 4, 1859, in Brooklyn, New York, filed for a widow's pension to help alleviate the burden she endured caring for their three children, Catharine, Mary Elizabeth, and Joseph.[31]

Edward Mullen (private)

On September 9, 1862, twenty-four-year-old Edward Mullen enlisted in the regiment. He was promoted to corporal on July 30, 1863. Wounded at Cool Spring, Mullen was sent to a hospital in Sandy Hook, Maryland. Mullen died ten days later from complications related to the amputation of his left foot and ankle. His mother, Margaret Mullen, filed for and received a pension of $8 per month.[32]

Lynden Parker (private)

A farmer, Parker enlisted in the 5th New York Heavy Artillery

---

[29] Thomas Lantry, 5th New York Heavy Artillery, CSR, NARA; Thomas Lantry, 5th New York Heavy Artillery, WP, NARA.
[30] Charles H. Mallory, 5th New York Heavy Artillery, CSR, NARA; Charles H. Mallory, 5th New York Heavy Artillery, MPR, NARA.
[31] Alexander McClure, 5th New York Heavy Artillery, CSR, NARA; Alexander McClure, 5th New York Heavy Artillery, WP, NARA.
[32] Edward Mullen, 5th New York Heavy Artillery, CSR, NARA; Edward Mullen, 5th New York Heavy Artillery, MPR, NARA.

on January 5, 1864. He was killed at Cool Spring.[33]

Nathan B. Sauter (private)

On February 23, 1864, twenty-five-year-old Sauter enlisted in the 5th New York Heavy Artillery at Brooklyn, New York. He was killed at Cool Spring.[34]

Abraham Sears (private)

Abraham Sears was born in 1829 in Rockland, New York. In the years prior to the conflict he worked as a brickmaker in New York City. He enlisted in the 5th New York Heavy Artillery in Brooklyn on November 23, 1863.[35] Sears was killed in action at the Battle of Cool Spring.[36]

Jacob W. Smith (private)

Jacob W. Smith was born in 1844 in Huntington, Long Island, New York. He worked as farmer prior to the conflict. He mustered into Company C, 5th New York Heavy Artillery on August 26, 1862. On July 18, 1864, Smith was killed at Cool Spring. He is buried in Green-Wood Cemetery in Brooklyn, Kings County, New York.[37]

Raymond Wade (private)

Raymond Wade was born in 1844 in Elmira, New York. He worked as a farmer for most of his life leading up to the war. Wade mustered into Company C as a private on October 2, 1862. According to his enlistment form, Wade had "black hair, brown eyes, and a dark complexion." Wade was killed in action at Cool Spring. The location of his remains is unknown.[38]

---

[33] *Annual Report of the Adjutant General of the State of New York*, 474; Lynden Parker, 5th New York Heavy Artillery, Abstracts from Original Muster Rolls for New York State Infantry Units Involved in the Civil War, New York State Archives, Albany, NY.
[34] *Annual Report of the Adjutant General of the State of New York*, 536.
[35] Abraham Sears Abstract Muster Roll, New York Civil War Muster Roll Abstracts, 1861-1900, New York State Archives, Albany, NY.
[36] *Annual Report of the Adjutant General of the State of New York*, 547.
[37] Jacob W. Smith, 5th New York Heavy Artillery, CSR, NARA; Jacob W. Smith, 5th New York Heavy Artillery, MPR, NARA.
[38] Raymond Wade Abstract Muster Roll, New York Civil War Muster Roll Abstracts, 1861-1900, New York State Archives, Albany, NY; *Annual Report of the Adjutant General of the State of New York*, 633.

Amos Wilcox (private)

Amos Wilcox was born in Steuben County, New York. A thirty-four-year-old laborer, Wilcox mustered into Company C on March 10, 1864. He was described as having "a fair complexion, brown hair, [and] blue eyes." Wilcox was killed at Cool Spring.[39]

11th West Virginia Infantry

Benjamin F. Jones (corporal)

Benjamin F. Jones was born in 1843 in Marion County, Virginia (West Virginia). Prior to the war, he was a laborer. He mustered into the regiment on August 31, 1862, in Parkersburg, West Virginia. He married Mary M. Dill on December 14, 1863. They had one child, a son, however Jones never had a chance to meet him. Jones' son was born on November 1, 1864.[40] The whereabouts of Corporal Jones' remains are unknown, but a letter in his widow's pension file notes that that "he was buried at or near where he was killed."[41]

Joseph McClintock (private)

Joseph McClintock was born in Ohio County, Virginia (West Virginia) in 1834, where he worked as a farmer in the years before the war. On August 18, 1862, at the age of twenty-eight, he enlisted in Company D, 11th West Virginia Infantry in Ravenswood, Virginia (West Virginia). McClintock was killed at Cool Spring on July 18.[42]

15th West Virginia Infantry

Robert Bell (private)

Private Robert Bell was among the twenty-six men from the 15th West Virginia Infantry wounded at the Battle of Cool Spring; however, he did not survive his wound. Bell, a farmer, enlisted in the 15th West Virginia on March 29, 1864. At the Battle of Cool Spring Bell was shot in the left lung. His comrades evacuated him from the field and Private Bell was soon sent to a hospital in Frederick,

---

[39] Amos Wilcox, 5th New York Heavy Artillery, CSR, NARA; Amos Wilcox, 5th New York Heavy Artillery, MPR, NARA.
[40] Benjamin F. Jones, 11th West Virginia Infantry, CSR, NARA.
[41] Benjamin F. Jones, 11th West Virginia Infantry, WP, NARA.
[42] Joseph McClintock, 11th West Virginia Infantry, CSR, NARA.

Maryland, but succumbed to his severe wound on August 26, 1864. Bell was twenty-years-old at the time of his death. Initially, Bell was buried in Frederick, but later interred at Antietam National Cemetery, grave 2622.[43]

John Cunningham (private)

John Cunningham was born in Scotland in 1844. He moved to the United States at an unknown time and settled in Independence, Virginia (now West Virginia). He found work as a farmer in the years leading up to the war. He enlisted in the 15th West Virginia Infantry in Independence on August 23, 1862, and was mustered into service as a private for three-years- service on September 10, 1862, in Wheeling, Virginia (West Virginia). While on campaign, Cunningham was detached for service in the pioneer corps on April 3, 1864. He was killed at Cool Spring.[44]

Washington Hiatt (private)

Washington Hiatt was born in 1848 in Hampshire County, Virginia (West Virginia). He worked as a farmer prior to the conflict. On March 20, 1864, he travelled to Paw Paw, West Virginia, to enlist in the 15th West Virginia Infantry. He was mustered into the regiment on March 31, 1864, in Wheeling. During the regiment's retreat at Cool Spring on the night of July 18, he unknowingly stumbled into Parker's Hole, an extremely deep section of the Shenandoah River. According to his casualty sheet, Hiatt was presumed to have drowned in Parker's Hole while retreating. His remains are believed to still be at the bottom of the river.[45]

Thomas Moris (sometimes Morris) (lieutenant-colonel)

At the Civil War's outset Moris resided in Marshall County, Virginia (West Virginia). On October 7, 1861, Moris received a commission as captain in Company B, 7th West Virginia Infantry. For "meritorious conduct as captain" in the 7th West Virginia, Moris received a promotion to lieutenant colonel of the 15th West Virginia

---

[43] Robert Bell, 15th West Virginia Infantry, CSR, NARA; Steven R. Stotelmyer, *The Bivouacs of the Dead: The Story of Those Who Died at Antietam and South Mountain, With Histories and Rosters of Antietam, Washington, Mt. Olivet and Elmwood Cemeteries* (Baltimore, MD: Toomey Press, 1992), 98.
[44] John Cunningham, 15th West Virginia Infantry, CSR, NARA.
[45] Washington J. Hiatt, 15th West Virginia Infantry, CSR, NARA.

Infantry on December 4, 1862.[46] He served in that capacity until he was killed at the Battle of Cool Spring. Following his death, Morris' wife, Elizabeth, filed a claim for a widow's pension with the federal government. The government initially awarded her $30 per month to support her and her five children. She continued to receive a pension until her death in 1914. Moris is buried in grave 3905 in the Winchester National Cemetery. His tombstone reads merely "T.M., W.VA."[47]

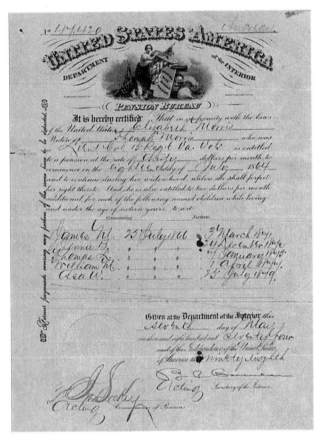

Document from Pension Bureau granting Elizabeth Morris a $30 per month pension following her husband's death at Cool Spring
(*Courtesy National Archives*)

---

[46] Theodore F. Lang, *Loyal West Virginia: From 1861 to 1865: With an Introductory Chapter on the Status of Virginia for Thirty Years Prior to the War* (Baltimore, MD: Deutsch Publishing Co., 1895), 298.
[47] Thomas Moris, 15th West Virginia Infantry, WP, NARA.

18th Connecticut Infantry

Thomas J. Aldrich (sergeant)

Thomas J. Aldrich was born in 1824, in Brooklyn, Connecticut. He married Ann M. Platt on September 4, 1853. Thomas and Ann had two children, eight-year-old Martha Helen Aldrich and three-year-old Mary Jane Aldrich. He enlisted in the 18th Connecticut on July 26, 1862, and mustered in on August 18, 1862, in Thompson, Connecticut. He eventually rose to the rank of sergeant. During the Union retreat at Cool Spring Aldrich was wounded and drowned in the Shenandoah River.[48] Aldrich is buried in West Thompson Cemetery, Thompson, Connecticut.[49]

John Carney (private)

A native of Windham, Connecticut, Carney enlisted in Company H, 18th Connecticut on August 9, 1862. Slightly more than two years after his enlistment he was killed at Cool Spring.[50]

John Delaney (private)

John Delaney enlisted in the 18th Connecticut Infantry on July 14, 1862, and mustered into service on August 18, 1862. What compelled him to enlist is uncertain, but some of his motivation might have stemmed from the fact that his father served in the Union army at the war's outset and was killed in 1861.[51] A bullet struck Delaney during the Union retreat at Cool Spring and he reportedly drowned in the river.[52]

Gabriel Hartford (corporal)

Gabriel Hartford, of Canterbury, Connecticut, enlisted in the 18th Connecticut Infantry on July 18, 1862. He mustered into Company A as a corporal on the same day. He held that rank at the time of his death at Cool Spring.[53] His remains were returned home and buried in Westminster Cemetery in Canterbury. After his

---

[48] Thomas J. Aldrich, 18th Connecticut Infantry, WP, NARA.
[49] Thomas J. Aldrich Tombstone, West Thompson Cemetery, Thompson, Windham County, Connecticut.
[50] William C. Walker, *History of the Eighteenth Regiment Connecticut Volunteers in the War for the Union* (Norwich, CT: Published by the Committee, 1885), 414.
[51] John Delaney, 18th Connecticut Infantry, WP, NARA.
[52] John Delaney, 18th Connecticut Infantry, WP, NARA.
[53] Walker, *History of the Eighteenth*, 694.

death, his wife, Nanno, applied for a widow's pension. The couple married on March 28, 1861; they had one child, a daughter Gabriella. She was born on April 2, 1862. Nanno passed away on December 11, 1869. After Nanno's death, Gabriella filed for a minor's pension. She received $8 per month.[54]

James M. Smith (private)

In August 1862, twenty-year-old James M. Smith, a farmer born in Killingly, Connecticut, enlisted in the 18th Connecticut. He was captured at the Second Battle of Winchester on June 15, 1863. His brother Samuel was also captured at the battle. Both were paroled on July 14, 1863. Approximately two months after his enlistment, James penned a letter to his sister-in-law, Hannah Bastow Smith, in which he mused about the sorrow that the Civil War would bring to families. "There will be sorrow in some, if not all families," Smith wrote, "but those that are lucky will return and those that are not, their friends will not have cause to blush for them. For myself, I should choose, when my time comes to die, to die at home, but next to that, fighting for my country and flag."[55] Less than two-years later Smith died at the Battle of Cool Spring. Although official documents state that Smith was killed "by gun shot wound received in action at Snickers ford Va," his brother Samuel, positioned behind him during the retreat across the Shenandoah River on the evening of July 18, noted that although a Confederate bullet did indeed hit James, it was drowning in the Shenandoah River that ultimately killed James.[56] According to Samuel, the Shenandoah River's current carried James' body a few miles downstream where it was pulled out and buried in a temporary grave by a local resident. Samuel, however, did not allow his brother's remains to rest in perpetuity in Virginia. In a letter he penned to his wife, Hannah, from Harpers Ferry on April 9, 1865, Samuel explained, "My 4 months pay I shall keep a while so that if there is any chance to get poor Jimmy's body… I got 64 dollars."[57] Samuel eventually had his brother's body removed and interred in

---

[54] Gabriel Hartford, 18th Connecticut Infantry, WP, NARA.
[55] James M. Smith to Hannah Bastow Smith, October 13, 1862, Mike Smith private collection.
[56] James M. Smith, 18th Connecticut Infantry, CSR, NARA.
[57] Samuel Smith to Hannah Bastow Smith, April 9, 1865, Mike Smith private collection.

the Smith family cemetery in East Killingly, Connecticut.[58]

Private James Smith (left) and Private Samuel Smith (right)
(*Courtesy Mike Smith private collection*)

---

[58] Special thanks to descendant Mike Smith for making information from the family archives available for use.

Marcus J. Weeks (private)

Marcus J. Weeks enlisted in the 18th Connecticut Infantry August 4, 1862, at Eastford, Connecticut. He mustered into Company G on August 21, 1862 at Camp Aiken. He was killed at Cool Spring. After his death his wife, Laura, received a widow's pension for $8 per month. They had one daughter, Grace.[59]

34th Massachusetts Infantry

Edwin W. Barlow (private)

A farmer from West Brookfield, Massachusetts, Edwin W. Barlow enlisted as a private in the 34th Massachusetts Infantry at Worcester, Massachusetts, on July 21, 1862. Barlow was eighteen years old at the time of his enlistment. Two years later he was killed at Cool Spring. He is buried in the Winchester National Cemetery, grave 3716.[60]

Dwight Chickering (private)

Dwight Chickering was born in the small town of Pomfret, Connecticut, in 1843 and worked as a farmer for most of his early life. He enlisted in the 34th Massachusetts Infantry on July 17, 1862. At Cool Spring, Chickering was "killed in action by enemy musket shot." He was buried on the field immediately after the battle but was later reinterred in Old Spencer Cemetery in Spencer, Massachusetts.[61]

David F. Coats (private)

When Coats enlisted in Company F, 34th Massachusetts Infantry, on December 30, 1863, he listed his occupation as farmer. An official statement prepared after the Battle of Cool Spring noted that he was "shot through the heart" at the battle.[62]

54th Pennsylvania Infantry

Henry Druckemiller (private)

---

[59] Marcus J. Weeks, 18th Connecticut Infantry, CSR, NARA. Marcus J. Weeks, 18th Connecticut Infantry, MPR, NARA.
[60] Edwin W. Barlow, 34th Massachusetts Infantry, CSR, NARA.
[61] Dwight Chickering, CSR, NARA.
[62] David F. Coats, 34th Massachusetts Infantry, CSR, NARA.

Druckemiller enlisted in Company K, 54th Pennsylvania on December 13, 1861. The whereabouts of his remains are unknown.[63]

Joseph Francis (private)

Joseph Francis enlisted in the 54th Pennsylvania Infantry on June 14, 1861.[64] For reasons unclear he was placed "In arrest at Harpers Ferry from October 8, 1862- October 31, 1862."[65] Prior to the war he married Mary Elizabeth on July 15, 1855.[66] Together they had two children, Anne and Mary. Joseph was fatally wounded at the Battle of Cool Spring by a gunshot to the head. His daughter Anne was five-years-old at the time of death, while Mary was three.[67]

William Haney (private)

Haney, a farmer, married Mary Ann Young, on September 7, 1847. The couple had two children, James (born September 28, 1853) and Henrietta (born June 20, 1858). He mustered into the 54th Pennsylvania on January 1, 1864, in Cumberland, Maryland. Six months after entering service, Haney was killed at Cool Spring. His remains were recovered and buried in the Winchester National Cemetery, grave 641. His wife received a widow's pension of $8 per month until September 18, 1866, when her pension was increased by $4.[68]

Peter Hersch (private)

A resident of Somerset County, Pennsylvania, Peter Hersch was fifty-years-old at the time he mustered into the 54th Pennsylvania Infantry on February 27, 1862. Following his death at Cool Spring he was buried on the battlefield and later moved to the Winchester National Cemetery, grave 660. He was survived by his wife, Mary, who he married on March 22, 1835, and his children, William, Silas, and Mary Ann.[69]

---

[63] Samuel P. Bates, *History of Pennsylvania Volunteers, 1861-5* (Harrisburg, PA: B. Singerley State Printer, 1869), 2: 172.
[64] Joseph Francis, 54th Pennsylvania Volunteer Infantry, WP, NARA.
[65] Ibid.
[66] Joseph Francis and Mary Elizabeth Francis Marriage License, in ibid.
[67] Ibid.
[68] William Haney, 54th Pennsylvania Volunteer Infantry, WP, NARA.
[69] Peter Hersch, 54th Pennsylvania Volunteer Infantry, WP, NARA; Bates, *History of Pennsylvania Volunteers*, 2: 165.

Private Hersch's tombstone in the Winchester National Cemetery
(*Photo by Jonathan A. Noyalas*)

Demetrius A. Holder (private)

Demetrius A. Holder was born in 1842. Prior to the war, he resided with his family in Wilmore, Pennsylvania.[70] He worked as a blacksmith's apprentice. Presumably, he worked under his father, Jacob Holder, who was a master blacksmith. He also lived with his mother, Mari Holder, and two brothers, James (aged sixteen) and Isadore (aged nineteen). Holder was killed at Cool Spring.[71]

Edward J. Lohr (private)

Born in 1841, Lohr mustered into the 54th Pennsylvania on March 12, 1864. Evidence indicates that he was severely wounded at Cool Spring, evacuated from the field, and sent to a hospital in Frederick, Maryland. He succumbed to his wounds on August 9, 1864. He was initially buried in Mount Olivet Cemetery in Frederick, Maryland, but later interred in Slick Cemetery, located in Shade Township, Somerset County, Pennsylvania.[72]

---

[70] Demetrius A. Holder, 54th Pennsylvania Volunteer Infantry, CSR, NARA.
[71] Ibid.; Demetrius A. Holder, 54th Pennsylvania Volunteer Infantry, MPR, NARA.
[72] Bates, *History of Pennsylvania Volunteers*, 2: 149; Private Edward J. Lohr, accessed July 3, 2019, https://www.findagrave.com/memorial/82479334/edward-j_-lohr

George Noble (private)

George Noble was born on an unknown date in County Derry, Ireland (now County Londonderry, Northern Ireland). He married Jane Akens while in Ireland, and the couple moved to Philadelphia, Pennsylvania. Jane gave birth to Elizabeth, on December 27, 1858. Noble enlisted in the 3rd Pennsylvania Reserve Infantry on September 16, 1862, as a private. He was transferred to the 54th Pennsylvania Infantry on July 4, 1864. Two weeks later he was killed at Cool Spring. Jane applied for a widow's pension on August 5, 1865. She received a monthly pension until her death on December 4, 1888.[73]

116th Ohio Infantry

Joshua Farley (private)

Regarded by his comrades as "an excellent soldier and a fine man" Joshua Farley mustered into the 116th Ohio in September 1862, six months after his wife, Elizabeth, died. Farley was killed at Cool Spring, a little more than one month after his only daughter's fourth birthday. After Cool Spring, Lieutenant Ransom Griffin assumed the responsibility of serving as guardian for Farley's daughter, Mary Ellen. She ended up receiving an $8 per month pension from the federal government.[74] Beloved by his comrades, his company commander Captain H.L. Karr wrote that Farley "was as brave a soldier and as brave a patriot as ever shouldered a musket in defense of his country." Karr also noted that Farley's "comrades carefully and tenderly laid him in a soldier's grave, a few feet from where he fell." Farley's remains were eventually moved to the Winchester National Cemetery, grave 709.[75]

Samuel Hayes (private)

Samuel Hayes was born in Marietta, Ohio in 1845. He enlisted in the 116th Ohio Infantry on December 25, 1863, at the age of eighteen. Hayes was killed at Cool Spring. His remains were

---

[73] George Noble, 54th Pennsylvania Volunteer Infantry, CSR, NARA; George Noble, 54th Pennsylvania Volunteer Infantry, WP, NARA.
[74] Joshua Farley, 116th Ohio Infantry, WP, NARA.
[75] Thomas F. Wildes, *Record of the One Hundred and Sixteenth Regiment Ohio Infantry Volunteers in the War of the Rebellion* (Sandusky, OH: I.F. Mack & Bro., Printers, 1884), 133.

returned to Marietta, Ohio, and interred in Oak Grove Cemetery.[76]

George Lamp (musician)

Eighteen years old at the time of his enlistment on August 20, 1862, Lamp served as a musician in the 116th Ohio. Described by the regiment's Thomas Wildes as a "fine boy," Lamp was shot in the head at Cool Spring. Lamp is buried in the Winchester National Cemetery, grave 349.[77]

William Stoneman (private)

William Stoneman served in Company I. He was killed Cool Spring. Private Stoneman is buried in Winchester National Cemetery, grave 699.[78]

123rd Ohio Volunteer Infantry

Lafayette Dunn (private)

Eighteen-years-old at the time of his enlistment in the 123rd Ohio on August 19, 1862, Dunn was captured during Union general Robert H. Milroy's retreat from Winchester, Virginia, on June 15, 1863. Slightly more than one year later Dunn was killed at Cool Spring.[79]

Albert Ott (private)

On August 14, 1862, Albert Ott, twenty years old, enlisted in Company G, 123rd Ohio Volunteer Infantry. He was captured at the Second Battle of Winchester in June 1863. Thirteen months later Ott was killed at Cool Spring.[80]

Bower W. Schnebly (private)

Twenty-one years old at the time of his enlistment on August 17, 1862, Schnebly was listed as being killed at the Second

---

[76] *Official Roster of the Soldiers of the State of Ohio in the War of the Rebellion, 1861-1866* (Cincinnati: The Ohio Valley Press, 1888), 8: 187.
[77] Ibid., 8: 739; George Lamp, 116th Ohio Volunteer Infantry, CSR, NARA; Wildes, *Record of the One Hundred and Sixteenth Regiment*, 133.
[78] William Stoneman, 116th Ohio Volunteer Infantry, CSR, NARA; William Stoneman, 116th Ohio Volunteer Infantry, WP, NARA.
[79] *Official Roster of the Soldiers of the State of Ohio*, 8: 364.
[80] Ibid., 8: 373.

Battle of Winchester. Although he survived the Second Battle of Winchester, he was killed at Cool Spring.[81]

Harvey Stansberry (private)

In August 1862, Harvey Stansberry mustered into Company A, 123rd Ohio Volunteer Infantry. He was captured at the Second Battle of Winchester and killed slightly more than one year later at Cool Spring.[82]

David Terry (sergeant)

David Terry was born in 1832 in Marseilles, Ohio. He married Marry Ann Watson, of Hardin County, Ohio, on February 2, 1859. David and Mary had two children, Joseph (born December 11, 1859) and Lycurgus (born November 28, 1861).[83] Less than a year after his second child was born, Terry enlisted in the 123rd Ohio Volunteer Infantry on August 12, 1862. He mustered into service as a private at Camp Monroeville, Ohio, on September 24, 1862. Terry was promoted to first sergeant in Company A in the spring of 1863. During the Second Battle of Winchester, Terry was captured. One year later Terry was killed at Cool Spring. The precise location of his grave remains unknown, although the *Official Roster of the Soldiers of the State of Ohio*, published in 1888, notes that he is buried in Winchester, presumably the Winchester National Cemetery. An examination of lists of burials for the cemetery, however, does not show that he is buried there. More than likely, he rests in an unknown grave in Winchester National Cemetery.[84] In his regimental history, Charles M. Keyes, wrote about Terry's mortal wounding and death. Referred to by Keyes as "Davis" (not to be confused with John Davis who was wounded in the head at Cool Spring, but survived), he wrote that Sergeant Terry was mortally wounded while "firing the last shot at the enemy." He was carried to Parker's Island where he was left to die. Keyes wrote that "before his brave spirit winged its flight to that other camping ground" Terry hid his personal belongings under a log so that they would

---

[81] Charles M. Keyes, *The Military History of the 123d Regiment Ohio Volunteer Infantry* (Sandusky, OH: Register Steam Press, 1874), 176; *Official Roster of the Soldiers of the State of Ohio*, 8: 356.
[82] *Official Roster of the Soldiers of the State of Ohio*, 8: 353.
[83] David Terry, 123rd Ohio Volunteer Infantry, WP, NARA.
[84] *Official Roster of the Soldiers from the State of Ohio*, 8: 350, 763.

not be stolen by Confederates.[85]

Immediately after her husband's death, Mary Ann Terry applied for a widow's pension. She initially received $8 per month. The monthly payments she received increased to $50 per month by the time of her death on March 29, 1929. After her death, her son Joseph petitioned the state of Ohio to use her upcoming pension money to pay for her burial expenses. After dozens of letters and heated debates, the state of Ohio finally gave in, covering the $270 worth of burial expenses for Mary Ann Terry.[86]

Lewis White (private)

Lewis White was born in Huron County, Ohio, in 1839. He enlisted in Company C, 123rd Ohio Volunteer Infantry on August 15, 1862. White was mustered in as the fifth sergeant of Company C on September 29, 1862, in Monroeville, Ohio. White was demoted from sergeant to private on December 31, 1863, for unknown reasons. During the Union retreat at Cool Spring, White drowned in the Shenandoah River. After his death, his wife, Barbara, applied for a widow's pension. Records do not clearly indicate if she ever received any compensation.[87] White is buried in Steuben, Ohio.[88]

Caleb D. Williams (first lieutenant)

Caleb Dayton Williams of Monroeville, Ohio, enlisted in the 123rd Ohio Volunteer Infantry September 1, 1863 in Martinsburg, West Virginia. He was thirty-two-years-old at the time he mustered into the regiment. After he was killed at Cool Spring, his wife, Cordelia, received a widow's pension of $17 per month to support her and her son. Williams in buried in Riverside Cemetery, Monroeville, Ohio.[89]

170th Ohio Volunteer Infantry

George Harper (private)

---

[85] Keyes, *The Military History of the 123d Regiment*, 79-80.
[86] David Terry, 123rd Ohio Volunteer Infantry, WP, NARA.
[87] *Official Roster of the Soldiers from the State of Ohio*, 8:357.
[88] Lewis White, 123rd Ohio Volunteer Infantry, CSR, NARA; Lewis White, 123rd Ohio Volunteer Infantry, WP, NARA.
[89] Caleb D. Williams, 123rd Ohio Infantry, CSR, NARA; Caleb D. Williams, 123rd Ohio Infantry, WP, NARA.

George Harper was born in Harrison County, Ohio. He enlisted in Company B, of the 170th Ohio on May 13, 1864, for a period of one hundred days. Harper was killed at Cool Spring by a gunshot wound to his head. His mother, Mary A. Harper, received a pension for $8 per month.[90]

James Haverfield (private)

Twenty-seven-year-old James Haverfield, of Harrison County, Ohio, enlisted as a corporal in the 170th Ohio on May 2, 1864, in Bellaire, Ohio. He mustered into service on May 13.[91] A comrade noted that at Cool Spring, Haverfield "offered up his young life, being shot and killed instantly." Haverfield's cousin Nathan was also a soldier in the 170th OVI, and witnessed James' death. Nathan, "aided by a comrade, carried him to the rear and across the river, and there they laid him to rest in a small garden, where his remains now sleep in an unknown grave."[92]

Colonel Samuel Young's Dismounted Cavalry

William H. Cushman, 2nd Ohio Cavalry (private)

Cushman enlisted in the 2nd Ohio Cavalry on January 1, 1864, and mustered in the same day. In a letter written to Cushman's wife, Mary, after Cushman was killed at Cool Spring, Sergeant G.W. Byard described how William died. He explained how fatigued they were from marching and that when they finally reached the Shenandoah River they were "surprised by the enemy and driven toward the river in great confusion." He told Mary that following their retreat to a barrier "made of stone and rails," Cushman was struck by "a bullet from the enemy... in the head and he died immediately." The bullet "entered just above his right eye and exited the back of his head." Byard assured Mary that her husband was "a good soldier, loved and respected by his comrades." Byard offered his "sincerest sympathies." Near the end of the letter Byard explained that "your husband fell in a good cause fighting the enemy of his country and received a decent burial at our hands." In a postscript following his signature, he let Mary know that her

---

[90] George Harper, 170th Ohio Volunteer Infantry, CSR, NARA; George Harper, 170th Ohio Volunteer Infantry, MPR, NARA.
[91] James Haverfield, CSR, NARA.
[92] *Official Roster of the Soldiers from the State of Ohio*, 8: 429.

husband's grave is "located on the South bank of the river about a mile below the ferry and Snickers Gap."[93] After the war Cushman was reinterred in Winchester National Cemetery, grave 792.

William McKinney, 1st Massachusetts Cavalry (sergeant)

William McKinney was born in Readville, Massachusetts, in 1839. He enlisted in the 1st Massachusetts Cavalry in Chelsea, Massachusetts, on January 5, 1864. McKinney mustered into service as a private on January 14 in Readville. Shortly after being mustered into service he was promoted to fifth sergeant. According to company muster rolls, McKinney was absent from the company due to sickness from March to June 1864. About one month after his return he was killed at Cool Spring.[94]

William W. Wright, 5th United States Cavalry (private)

A native of Waupaca County, Wisconsin, Wright enlisted in the 5th U.S. Cavalry on March 11, 1864. As part of Colonel Samuel Young's detachment of dismounted cavalry, Wright and his comrades were the first to feel the weight of Confederate general Robert Rodes' flank attack at Cool Spring. Several months after the battle, one of his comrades, A.W. Stumpe, penned a letter to Wright's widow, Mary, describing the moment of Private Wright's death:

> *Camp Stoneman*
> *Sep. 27, [1864]*

> *Whe [sic] where [sic] in charge of Col. Young... on the 18th day of July whe [sic] crossed the Shenandoah River near Snickers Gap at 4 o'clock P.M. and fought 3 hours. He [Private William Wright] was lying the seckond [sic] man from me behind a stone fence, I saw him raise to shoot when the fatal bullet took him in the head and caused his instant death. Whe [sic] were driven across the River and had to leave all our dead and wounded in the Rebel hands. I was very sorrow for poor Wright he was a good soldier and gentleman, as well as a good Christian and I hope he*

---

[93] William H. Cushman, 2nd Ohio Cavalry, WP, NARA.
[94] William McKinney, CSR, NARA.

is in a better World than this.

A.W. Stumpe

In addition to his wife, Wright also left behind three children—Edith (born August 3, 1860), Wallace (born December 9, 1861), and Mary (born March 25, 1864).[95]

---

[95] Private William W. Wright, 5th United States Cavalry, WP, NARA.

"Battery G Soon Made it Uncomfortable for the Rebels that They Ceased Firing"
Battery G, First Rhode Island Light Artillery and the Opening of the 1864 Valley Campaign

Robert Grandchamp

In the summer and fall of 1864, the men of the Army of the Potomac's Sixth Corps took part in the brutal fighting in the Shenandoah Valley. In engagements at Cool Spring, Opequon, Fisher's Hill, and their famous and desperate stand at Cedar Creek, the men who wore the Greek cross proved time and again that they were among the best troops in the Union army. In every one of those engagements, the federals' ability to bring accurate, pin point artillery fire to bear on the Confederates proved to be a decisive factor in the Union victory. One of the units that supported the Sixth Corps in the Shenandoah Valley was Battery G, First Rhode Island Light Artillery.

Raised in the fall of 1861, Battery G was the eighth battery of the First Rhode Island Light Artillery recruited in as many months. The unit was a distinct blend of Irish and German immigrants, merchants from Providence, as well as farmers and mill workers from southern Rhode Island. These groups all blended seamlessly to work the cannon of the battery. As part of the Second Corps, Battery G was baptized at Yorktown in April 1862, later fighting at Fair Oaks and Malvern Hill during the Peninsula Campaign. Heavily engaged near the Dunker Church at Antietam, Battery G also was present at Fredericksburg in a supporting role. On May 3, 1863, at the Second Battle of Fredericksburg, as part of the Chancellorsville Campaign, Battery G supported the Sixth Corps in the storming of Marye's Heights. Sent out early to distract the Confederates, the men of Battery G were caught in the open by Confederate batteries, resulting in seven deaths and twenty men wounded; high losses for any battery. After refitting, Battery G was transferred to the Sixth Corps in June 1863, where they remained for the war's duration. Although present at Gettysburg, the battery took part in only a small skirmish near Fairfield on July 5, 1863. In the spring of 1864, Battery G supported the Sixth Corps at Spotsylvania Court House, and was later heavily engaged at Cold Harbor. With the rest of the Army of the Potomac, the Rhode Islanders arrived at Petersburg in mid-June 1864, tired and worn out, but hopeful that the Army of Northern Virginia was finally trapped.[1]

Battery G was commanded by Captain George W. Adams of Providence. Son of a wealthy and politically well-connected merchant, Adams owed his position to his unrivaled experience commanding artillery in action. Before the war, Adams, then a student at Brown University, like many members of the First Rhode Island Light Artillery, was a member of the Rhode Island Militia, serving in the Providence Marine Corps of Artillery, where he learned the intricacies of field artillery drill. After a three-month stint in the First Rhode Island Battery, he became a first lieutenant in Battery B, First Rhode Island Light Artillery, serving at Ball's Bluff, the Peninsula, Antietam, and Fredericksburg, where he was cited for bravery under fire. Promoted to captain, Adams arrived at Battery G only twelve hours before their participation at Second Fredericksburg. Universally respected by his men, Captain Adams was one of the most proficient gunners in the Army of the Potomac, and led his men into action in 1864.[2]

With his army pinned down in trench warfare, Robert E. Lee again prepared to steal the initiative as the two armies engaged in a death struggle around Petersburg. With the majority of the troops in the Washington defenses removed to join the Army of the Potomac, Confederate general Robert E. Lee felt the Confederates could make an attack down the Shenandoah Valley, threaten and even possibly capture the United States capital. With supply lines being stretched daily, this campaign would be the Confederates' last chance to win the war. He tapped Jubal Early, his sole remaining senior commander, who would lead the Second Corps down their

---

[1] For the most comprehensive history of Battery G, refer to Robert Grandchamp, *The Boys of Adams' Battery G: The Civil War through the Eyes of a Union Light Artillery Unit*. (Jefferson, NC: McFarland, 2009).

[2] John Russell Bartlett. *Memoirs of Rhode Island Officers, Who Were Engaged in the Service of Their Country During the Great Rebellion of the South: Illustrated with Thirty-Four Portraits*. (Providence: Sydney S. Rider, 1867), 414-418. *Providence Journal*, October 14, 1883.

former stomping grounds in the Valley. Timing was essential. Early had to reach Washington before federal reinforcements made it to the city. Early's force marched on June 19. By the first of July, the army was at Harpers Ferry and invaded the North for the third time during the war. The force was detained here for four days by a dogged federal resistance.³

Captain George W. Adams
(*Courtesy Robert Grandchamp private collection*)

When Grant finally learned of Early's movements he dispatched the Sixth Corps, mustering 12,000 men, to reinforce Washington. Originally, Grant ordered the Sixth's commander Horatio Wright to take only his infantry, leaving the artillery behind. Wright pleaded with Grant to have his batteries present, knowing full well that his artillery could play a decisive role in determining victory or defeat. Grant relented and permitted Wright to take the artillery. With these orders, Battery G, armed with four, three-inch ordnance rifled guns, proceeded north. They did so with reduced ranks; there were only three officers and 120 enlisted men on duty, ten men were absent sick or wounded. Corporal James

---

³ Jubal Early, "Early's March to Washington in 1864" in *Battles and Leaders of the Civil War* (New York: Thomas Yoseloff, Inc., 1956), 4: 492-499. John F. Ward to Mother and Father, June 30, 1864, Harpers Ferry National Historical Park, Harpers Ferry, WV.

Barber, a fisherman from Westerly had become ill in late June and was sent to a hospital in Washington; he was not excused from duty as every available man in the city was given a rifle to fend off the Confederate invasion.[4]

At 9 o'clock on the night of July 9, the Sixth Corps Artillery Brigade received orders to move to the City Point docks immediately; within an hour-and-a-half, the batteries were on their way to counter the threat. The artillery was commanded by Colonel Charles H. Tompkins, the chief of the Sixth Corps Artillery Brigade. Tompkins was also the regimental commander of the First Rhode Island Light Artillery. He had already left with the lead elements of the corps, so Captain James McKnight of the Fifth United States Artillery was placed in temporary command. Before the batteries were allowed to board the vessels, McKnight quickly rushed through the ordnance depot at City Point, finding every available artillerist he could. McKnight did not know what he faced to the north and wanted as many men in his batteries as could be mustered. Sixty men were found and sent to the Sixth Corps Artillery Brigade. Because of the hastiness of the situation, Captain Adams did not have time to record their names and most of them were sent back after the emergency was over. Battery G embarked on July 11 and hastened north.[5]

On July 9, Early was at Frederick, Maryland. Here General Lew Wallace cobbled together a defense, which included the Sixth Corps' third division, to slow Early's advance. Although defeated at the Battle of Monocacy, Wallace bought precious time for the Sixth Corps to arrive in Washington, as the remaining two divisions moved up the Chesapeake in an all-night rush up the bay. The greatly needed reinforcements arrived in Alexandria on July 12 and quickly disembarked. Battery G dashed through the streets of the city along with the rest of the Sixth Corps as they hurried to the forts north of the city. The citizens lined the streets, instantly recognizing the Greek crosses on the men's hats by shouting, "It's the old Sixth

---

[4] U.S. War Department, comp., *War of the Rebellion: A Compilation of the Official Records of the Union and Confederate Armies* (Washington, D.C.: Government Printing Office, 1880-1901), ser. 1, vol. 37, 282-283. Hereafter cited as *O.R.* James A. Barber Diary, July 1864, John Hay Library, Brown University, Providence, RI. Battery G, First Rhode Island Light Artillery, Monthly Return, July 1864, Rhode Island State Archives, Providence, RI.
[5] George Lewis, *The History of Battery E, First Regiment Rhode Island Light Artillery, in the War of 1861 and 1865, to Preserve the Union*. (Providence: Snow & Farnum, 1892), 339. Augustus C. Buell, *The Cannoneer* (Washington, D.C.: National Tribune, 1890), 263-264.

Corps. Those are the men who took Marye's Heights." Even local Maryland slaves knew what the Greek cross represented, for behind it marched men who knew no fear. Some dropped to their knees as the Artillery Brigade marched by, believing slavery's destruction had come in the form of men in short jackets trimmed in red and with thick Yankee accents.[6]

Colonel Charles Tompkins
(*Courtesy Robert Grandchamp private collection*)

Only a few hours later the Confederate force arrived in Washington. General Wright delivered his men in time to make a

---

[6] George T. Stevens, *Three Years in the Sixth Corps.* (New York: D. Van Nostrand, 1870), 372-374; Buell, *The Cannoneer,* 269-271.

difference as they marched to reinforce the forts north of the city. A sharp skirmish erupted at Fort Stevens as the Sixth Corps repulsed the Confederate attack. For Battery G the mad rush from Petersburg had been for naught. They were held in reserve and were not engaged. Indeed, none of the artillery was called for, as the infantry slugged it out. Finally, at dusk the Confederates broke off the assault and withdrew. Even though Early did not capture Washington, his push to D.C.'s outskirts raised anxieties in the nation's capital. If Early had attacked only a few hours earlier, he might have been successful. "Early was late," one Rhode Islander recorded.[7]

After being defeated, the Confederate force retreated towards Virginia. Lincoln demanded Early's army be pursued and destroyed. On the morning of July 13, as the Union pursuit force commanded by General Wright prepared to move, Corporal Augustus Buell of the Fifth United States Artillery noticed another in a long series of feuds between the Rhode Islanders of Batteries C and G and the First Massachusetts Battery. This time it was settled with a boxing match, but before it could be finished, orders came to move out. The cannoneers decided they would settle their differences elsewhere. Twenty-four hours after arriving in Washington, Battery G left Fort Stevens and hurried after the Confederates. Before the Sixth Corps Artillery Brigade departed, Colonel Tompkins reduced his forces, as the guns were desperately needed at Petersburg. Of the nine batteries in the brigade, three were sent back, Captain William B. Rhodes and Battery E among them. In addition, Tompkins divided his brigade so each infantry division would have one smoothbore and one rifled battery assigned to it. Battery G now marched as part of the Sixth Corps' third division.[8]

With the Confederates in full retreat towards the Potomac, the Sixth Corps marched towards Leesburg to cut them off. This area was intimately familiar to the original members of Battery G, having served here in the early part of 1862 as raw recruits. On July 15, a small portion of Early's force was detected near Poolesville, Maryland, as they raced to Virginia, only ten miles away. The

---

[7] O.R., ser. 1, vol. 37, 282-283; Elisha Hunt Rhodes, *All for the Union: The Civil War Diary and Letters of Elisha Hunt Rhodes* (Woonsocket, RI: Andrew Mowbray, 1985), 160-163.
[8] Buell, *The Cannoneer*, 274-277; Kris VanDen Bossche, *Please Excuse All Bad Writing: A Documentary History of Rhode Island During the Civil War Era, 1854-1865* (Peace Dale, RI: Historical Document Transcription Project, 1993), 192-194.

Sixteenth Pennsylvania Cavalry was ordered to charge into the rearguard and drive them into the Potomac. They were to be supported by a section from Battery G. Captain Adams ordered his right section, commanded by First Lieutenant Elmer Corthell to engage. The charge was successful, as the Confederates ran for their lives, while a Baltimore battery engaged the force. Lieutenant Corthell promptly unlimbered his section and fired twenty-seven rounds. Corthell cleared the town and drove away any remaining Confederates. When it ended, the last Confederate invasion of the North was finally over.[9]

Battery G was ordered to remain behind as the rearguard as most of the Sixth Corps moved ahead and crossed the Potomac on the 16th; Adams' Battery crossed the following day. They were back in Virginia after a five-day foray in Maryland. Meanwhile General Horatio Wright pressed his men hard and ordered the Sixth Corps into the Shenandoah Valley. On the 18th, Battery G and the 121st New York passed through Purcellville and Snickers Gap as the Sixth Corps continued on with its mission to locate and destroy the Confederate army. On the afternoon of July 18, the Confederates were located on the west bank of the Shenandoah River.[10]

From this position Jubal Early controlled the vital crossing, Castleman's Ford. Early hoped for a rearguard action as his forces withdrew in the face of superior numbers. This was exactly what he had done one year earlier at Granite Hill, after Gettysburg. Around 3 o'clock in the afternoon on July 18, Colonel Joseph Thoburn's division of General George Crook's Eighth Corps, forded the Shenandoah River, initially coming under fire from the 42nd Virginia Infantry. The lead elements of Thoburn's division, Colonel George Wells' brigade, drove the Virginians off. However, the musket fire that erupted along the banks of the Shenandoah River near Island Ford prompted Early to send two Confederate divisions toward Cool Spring. Portions of Thoburn's command fled when Confederate general Robert Rodes' division struck Thoburn's left flank. With the troops who remained, and without any support,

---

[9] *O.R.*, vol. 37, 282-283; Robert J. Trout, *Galloping Thunder: The Stuart Horse Artillery Battalion*, (Mechanicsburg, PA: Stackpole Books, 2002), 534-545.
[10] *O.R.*, vol. 37, 282-283; James B. Ricketts, Third Division, Sixth Corps, Memoranda Book, July 18, 1864, Manassas National Battlefield, Manassas, VA. Hereafter cited as MNB. The Shenandoah River flows north, emptying into the Potomac at Harpers Ferry. Traveling south is therefore called "going up the Valley."

Thoburn shuffled his regiments as best he could. His men constructed a makeshift barricade behind a stone wall, fending off their attackers, all the while looking to the east, waiting for reinforcements to arrive.

At 6:00 p.m., as the Thoburn's line seemed to be crumbling, support finally appeared in the form of the Sixth Corps. However, by that point General Wright decided against bringing on a large battle, so instead of making good on his initial promise to General Crook that he would send General James Ricketts' division across the Shenandoah River, Wright kept Ricketts on the river's eastern shore to lay down a covering fire, as Robert Rodes' division approached to within 100 yards of the thin blue line. As this occurred, Confederate artillery from the Monroe Artillery began shelling the advancing Union regiments with a pair of twenty pound Parrotts. Wright now turned to Colonel Charles Tompkins.[11]

Immediately, Tompkins took command of the situation. There was a large, wide open hill overlooking the ford where Battery E, First West Virginia Light Artillery had already been stationed with their four Napoleons. The Rhode Island colonel knew it was the perfect position to place his guns and called for his two favorite batteries. It was difficult work getting the guns up the ridge, but time was of the essence, and with the Confederates almost right on top of Thoburn's men, there was no time to waste. The Rhode Islanders and some New Yorkers strained every muscle in their bodies to get the four ten pounder Parrotts of Battery C to the right of the crest, and the four ordnance rifles of Battery G to the left of the West Virginians. The men did not hesitate and quickly brought the guns into action. Captain Adams realized that he had to be extremely careful. With the enemy only five hundred yards away and firing over the head of friendly infantry, his number six men would have to be precise in the cutting of the fuses. Meanwhile the gunners would have to take steady aim to be sure of their targets. Finally, all was in order as Adams barked out the command to open fire.[12]

---

[11] John F. Ward to Mother and Father, July 21, 1864, Harpers Ferry National Historical Park, Harpers Ferry, WV; Thomas F. Wildes, *Record of the One Hundred and Sixteenth Regiment Ohio Volunteers in the War of the Rebellion* (Sandusky: I.F. Mack, 1884), 129-131; Scott C. Patchan, *Shenandoah Summer: The 1864 Valley Campaign*. (Lincoln: University of Nebraska Press, 2007), 60-89.

[12] Peter J. Meaney, *The Civil War Engagement at Cool Spring, July 18, 1864: The Largest Battle*

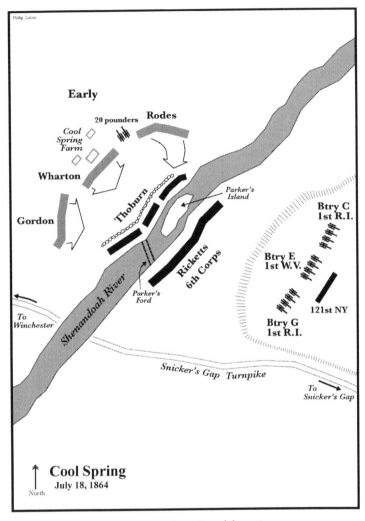

(Courtesy Robert Grandchamp)

A correspondent for the *Washington Chronicle* attached to the Sixth Corps described what happened next:

> *At this critical moment, Adams' Rhode Island Battery came into position on an eminence overlooking the valley*

ever fought in Clark County, Virginia. (Berryville, VA: Meaney, 1979), 32-33. As was the case of every battle fought by Battery G, this author has visited and walked each site and can attest to the difficulty in bringing artillery up this ridge.

below. They immediately opened upon the enemy with shot and shell from three inch rifled guns, creating great havoc among them. The range was very accurate, and each shell burst in their midst. The enemy finding the damage to their infantry so great, attempted to silence the battery by firing upon them with twenty pound Parrotts, which however lasted, but a moment, as they in turn were fired upon and forced to cease. The scene was a most exciting one; generals, colonels and others were standing near, and high compliments were passed on to this battery by General Russell and others. The writer of this met this command at Fort Stevens; and having, some experience in military matters could not fail to admire their soldierly appearance, and felt assured that if an opportunity occurred during the campaign, they would distinguish themselves.[13]

The cannonade from the heavy Parrott rifles had no effect on Battery G. The rounds flew overhead, landing in the ranks of the New Yorkers posted to the battery's rear. Among Thoburn's regiments was the Eighteenth Connecticut, a unit recruited along the Rhode Island border. Now down to sixty men, they finally received the miracle for which they had been hoping. Chaplain William C. Walker wrote, "A rebel battery opened upon the Union force with some effect, and would have done great harm if it had not been checkmated by a battery of the Sixth Corps, which by a well-directed shot blew up a rebel caisson." The actions of Battery G were becoming a scene of great interest to all who witnessed it. A Vermont officer on General Ricketts' staff wrote, "Batteries were at once placed in position and the Enemy were shelled + their advance checked." Other soldiers watched the spectacle occurring on the banks of the Shenandoah River. Captain Elisha Rhodes of the Second Rhode Island recalled, "Battery G soon made it uncomfortable for the Rebels that they ceased firing." General Wright dispatched the 37th Massachusetts and the 2nd Rhode Island to support the third division. These two regiments had recently been armed with the new seven-shot Spencer rifle. This added even more support to keep the Confederates away from the stone wall

---

[13] Bartlett, *Memoirs of Rhode Island*, 415-416; *Providence Journal*, July 27, 1864.

and the remaining Union survivors. Despite this added firepower, the Bay Staters were still amazed at the support coming from Adams' Rhode Island Battery. James L. Bowen wrote, "They were punished by the Union batteries on the opposite hills."[14]

Captain Elisha Hunt Rhodes
(Courtesy Robert Grandchamp private collection)

---

[14] William C. Walker, *History of the Eighteenth Connecticut Volunteers in the War for the Union* (Norwich, CT: Gordon Wilcox, 1886), 286-288; Ricketts, Memoranda Book, July 18, 1864; MNB; Rhodes, *All for the Union*, 165-169; James L. Bowen, *History of the Thirty-Seventh Regiment, Mass. Volunteers, in the Civil War of 1861-1865: With a Comprehensive Sketch of the Doings of Massachusetts as a State, and of the Principal Campaigns of the War* (Holyoke, MA: C.W. Bryan & Co., 1884), 362-364.

The firepower of the three-inch ordnance rifles of Battery G and the ten pounder Parrotts of Battery C were having their effect on General Rodes' division. The earlier problems the battery encountered with the Dyer and Hotchkiss ammunition at Antietam and First Fredericksburg had largely disappeared as the ammunition worked exactly as it was supposed to at Cool Spring. Each round of Hotchkiss shell and case was fired precisely and timed to perfection to burst in the midst of the Confederates. Corporal Edward Adams of Battery G remembered it as, "a most destructive fire." A member of the Fourth North Carolina, on the receiving end, described the bombardment as "a deadly fire into our ranks with impunity." Although the cannonade slowed Rodes' attack, the closeness of the Union and Confederate lines proved worrisome for some federal commanders on the west bank of the river. The 116th Ohio's Lieutenant Colonel Thomas F. Wildes observed, "The lines were so close to each other that some damage to our own men was caused by shells from our batteries. But they kept the rebels discretely under cover." Sergeant John Hartwell of New York wrote, "Our batteries made terrible havock of the enemys [sic] line & forced them to seek cover under hills & stonewalls."[15]

As night came on, the artillery on both sides, including Battery G, continued the barrage; the only light being the muzzle flashes of the cannon, which allowed the gunners to hone in on their targets. With artillery and darkness as their ally, the surviving federals successfully crossed the river. Early had hoped for another Ball's Bluff, where the Union command was destroyed as it crossed the river. This battle in October 1861, which involved Battery B, was a distinct embarrassment to the Union cause in the wake of Bull Run. However, it was not 1861 and two Rhode Island batteries would not let it occur as they continued their work into the darkness. Finally, around 9:00 p.m. the Battle of Cool Spring concluded. Early withdrew the following day and Wright did not pursue.

In the engagement, Battery G fired a total of 134 rounds. Federal casualties were 422 to 397 Confederates. In the aftermath of the battle, Chaplain Alanson Haines of the 15th New Jersey attended

---

[15] Clarence R. Geier and Stephen R. Potter, eds., *Archaeological Perspectives on the American Civil War* (Gainesville: University Press of Florida, 2003) 73-93; O.R., vol. 37, 283; Wildes, *One Hundred and Sixteenth*, 131; John F. L. Hartwell, Ann H. Britton, and Thomas J. Reed, *To My Beloved Wife and Boy at Home: The Letters and Diaries of Orderly Sergeant John F.L. Hartwell* (Madison, NJ: Fairleigh Dickinson University Press, 1997), 257.

to the dead and wounded and observed in reference to the Union casualties, "Losses were four hundred men, and those of the enemy must have been also large, as they were exposed to our batteries, and the next day were observed burying their slain."[16]

Even though the Rhode Islanders saved the day during the daylight hours, at night it became a bit of an annoyance for some Union soldiers, trying to rest amid the cannonade and the occasional picket shot as the artillery rounds overshot Battery G and landed in a field to the rear of the hill. Chaplain Edward M. Haynes of the Tenth Vermont wrote, "The scene closed for the night with an artillery duel conducted from low commanding ridges on opposite banks of the river, very much to the annoyance of our infantry which had been dropped into an open field stretching back behind the ridge occupied by our batteries."[17]

For Battery G, the Battle of Cool Spring was a supreme victory. The artillerists were able to use their guns effectively as an offensive weapon to help the beleaguered Union forces from being overwhelmed by a vastly superior foe. This enabled Thoburn's brigades to hold on until darkness. Indeed, one historian of the battle argued that without the artillery support, the federal regiments would have been driven into the Shenandoah. Relating to Battery G's role, he wrote, "George W. Adams' Battery G went into position on an eminence behind the ford and soon it began to find the mark just at the right moment." A careful review of a dozen sources from Union infantrymen who fought at Cool Spring, both from Thoburn's men on the west bank of the Shenandoah and those of the Sixth Corps who did not cross, are all unanimous in one regard—without the support of Batteries C and G, First Rhode Island Light Artillery, Thoburn's Division would have been annihilated.[18]

Wright bivouacked the Sixth Corps along the Blue Ridge on the night of the 18th, but during the night, a Confederate battery reappeared and shelled the line, causing it to be moved in the middle of the night. The Rhode Islanders were exhausted after the battle. In forty-eight hours, Battery G marched over sixty miles. The

---

[16] Patchan, *Shenandoah Summer*, 87-104; Alanson Haines, *History of the Fifteenth Regiment New Jersey Volunteers* (New York: Jenkins & Thomas, Printers, 1883), 229-230.
[17] Edward M. Haynes, *A History of the Tenth Regiment Vermont Volunteers* (Lewiston, ME: Journal Steam Press, 1870), 90-92.
[18] Meaney, *Cool Spring*, 32.

hard packed macadam roads in Maryland and the Shenandoah contributed to the artillerists' misery as their shoes and those of the horses were worn out. "The men were plaid [sic] out as ever," recalled a member of the Second Rhode Island.[19]

Two days after the Battle of Cool Spring, Union general William Averell defeated a portion of Early's army commanded by General Stephen D. Ramseur at the Battle of Rutherford's Farm, located a few miles north of Winchester. That Union victory, coupled with reports that Early's command was in the process of leaving the Valley to support the Army of Northern Virginia's operations around Petersburg, prompting General Ulysses S. Grant to order the Sixth Corps back to Petersburg. Early, however, had no intention of leaving the Valley. After Early's army delivered a crushing blow to the remaining Union forces in the Shenandoah Valley, Crook's Eighth Corps, on July 24 at the Second Battle of Kernstown, Confederate general John McCausland's cavalry dashed north across the Potomac. On July 30, McCausland burned Chambersburg, Pennsylvania, in retaliation for Union destruction in the Valley. With Early still in the Valley, Grant ordered the Sixth Corps back. They rendezvoused near Harpers Ferry, West Virginia. Battery G had last visited the area after Antietam, camping for a month on Bolivar Heights. Captain Adams moved the command two miles west of the Ferry to Halltown, a small community that guarded the roads to Charles Town and Sharpsburg.[20]

Battery G remained at Harpers Ferry throughout August. During the first week of August, General Philip H. Sheridan arrived and took command of the newly-established Middle Military Division. He had already made a name for himself in the war's western theater and in command of the Army of the Potomac's Cavalry Corps. Now Sheridan took command of the largest Union army ever assembled in the Shenandoah Valley, a force of approximately 40,000 soldiers from the Sixth, Eighth, Nineteenth, and Cavalry Corps. Throughout August, the men of Battery G waited, reequipped with new uniforms and new horses, and

---

[19] Charles E. Perkins to Sister, July 30, 1864, U.S. Army Heritage and Education Center, Carlisle, PA.
[20] Rhodes, *All for the Union*, 165-169; John W. Chase, John S. Collier, and Bonnie B. Collier. *Yours for the Union: The Civil War Letters of John W. Chase, First Massachusetts Light Artillery* (Ashland, OH: Fordham University Press, 2004), 160-163; Bartlett, *Memoirs of Rhode Island*, 415.

prepared their guns for action. Ahead lay the bloody fields of Opequon, Fisher's Hill, and Cedar Creek.[21]

---

[21] Chase, *Yours for the Union,* 357-363; Battery G, Monthly Return, August 1864, Rhode Island State Archives, Providence, RI; Battery G, Clothing Book, Rhode Island Historical Society, Providence, RI; *O.R.,* ser. 1, vol. 36, 771-772; *O.R.,* ser. 1, vol. 37, 282; *O.R.,* ser. 1, vol. 40, 521.

"In Order that He May Have the Opportunity to Attend School and Fit Himself for the Duties of a Free Man"
Reforming Black Minors' Labor in the Post-Emancipation Shenandoah Valley[1]

Donna Dodenhoff

In the Civil War's aftermath, as African Americans in the Shenandoah Valley withdrew from white households and formed their own independent ones, claiming their children from the youths' former masters and mistresses advanced the freedpeople's efforts to gain greater control over their families' living and work arrangements. Only by asserting their guardianship rights could the freedpeople prevent whites' unfettered access to their children's labor and offer them a better future in the post-emancipation Shenandoah Valley. Only by claiming their children from white households could freedpeople begin healing one of slavery's most egregious wounds—the arbitrary separation of family members through the slave trade.

In 1866 the Virginia legislature acknowledged the importance of reunited black families to the Commonwealth's post-emancipation social order by passing the Cohabitation Act, a law that gave legal status to the partnerships African Americans had formed in slavery. Legally protected family units encouraged a responsible work ethic among the freedpeople and supported the societal stability afforded by their family ties. The Freedmen's Bureau backed up the legislature's policy. General Oliver O.

---

[1] Captain John McDonnell, Winchester Freedmen's Bureau head, to Orlando Brown, head of the Virginia Bureau, in Richmond, October 23, 1868. Records of the Field Offices for the State of Virginia, Bureau of Refugees, Freedmen, and Abandoned Lands (hereafter BRFAL), 1865-1872, Accession. 44121, Misc. reel 5712, roll 187, frames 368-9.

Howard, Commissioner of the Freedmen's Bureau, stressed that "The unity of black families and all the rights of family relations were to be carefully guarded."[2]

While Freedmen's Bureau agents in areas of Virginia experiencing economic distress, such as Tidewater Virginia, were turning their backs as whites claimed guardianship of black youths without the consent of their families, in the Valley, Bureau agents considered the freedpeople's guardianship rights a charged civil rights issue. Labor arrangements the freedpeople made for their children with white employers had to be consensual and could be canceled if whites breached an agreement or mistreated their children.[3] Several months after the Civil War, in calling for the release of black children held by the Meades, a prominent Clarke County planter family, an indignant agent reported: "All the Meade family from the old Bishop to his youngest relations are vile rebels. Can they be permitted to retain these children? Are they to triumph over our ways?"[4]

In the Valley's resilient post-War farm economy many freedpeople were securing the employment they needed to convince Bureau agents that they had sufficient income to provide their children with good homes. Yet progress in reforming the labor of black minors was not without its challenges. In the Civil War's chaotic aftermath whites who harbored black minors could put up

---

[2] Oliver Otis Howard, *Autobiography of Oliver Otis Howard: Major General United States Army* (New York: Baker & Taylor Company, 1867), 2: 223.

[3] The Richmond Freedmen's Bureau Circular No. 8 stated that apprenticeship contracts were valid only if they were made with the consent of black minors' nearest of kin. The agents applied this standard to less formal arrangements involving the labor of black minors as well. Records of the Field Offices for the State of Virginia, BRFAL, 1865-1872, Accession. 44121, Misc. reel 5716, roll 191, frame 183.

[4] August 31, 1865, communication of Captain How relating the story of freedpeople, formerly contraband of War, who had been slaves of the Meade family in Clarke County and were now resettled in Chambersburg, Pa. Captain How's indignation was somewhat misdirected. The "old bishop" he referred to, William Meade, the third Protestant Episcopal Bishop of Virginia, died during the conflict and, ironically, had been an anti-slavery proponent earlier in the century. Records of the Field Offices for the State of Virginia, BRFAL, 1865-1872, Accession. 44121, Misc. reel 5716, roll 191, frames 507-11. See Robert Engs on the more widespread practice of re-enslaving black minors by whites in Tidewater Virginia in "The Chaos of Peace," *Freedom's First Generation: Black Hampton, Virginia, 1861-1871* (Philadelphia: University of Pennsylvania Press, 1979), 97. On the use of the apprenticeship system to re-enslave black minors across the South, see Eric Foner, *Reconstruction: America's Unfinished Revolution: 1863-1877* (New York: Harper & Rowe, 1988), 201-202; Donald G. Nieman, *To Set the Law in Motion: The Freedmen's Bureau and the Legal Rights of Blacks, 1865-1868* (Millwood, NY: KTO Press, 1979), 78, 137-138.

strong resistance to the freedpeople's guardianship claims. The toll the slave trade had taken on black families meant that many black women entered freedom as struggling single mothers who had to find work for their children with white employers in order to keep their families together. Moreover, as the guardians of a large number of displaced black orphans, Freedmen's Bureau agents initially saw few options to averting a humanitarian disaster than having them apprenticed to white families or sent to the Orphanage for Colored Children in Washington, D. C. George Cook of Harrisonburg contacted the Winchester Bureau noting: "The difficulty seems to be that parents have been sold so far away that it is impossible to ascertain whether they were living or not. In many instances it seems to me that the best thing that could be done for the children would be to bind them out."[5]

With the Civil War's end, the emancipation of many black youths began when their guardians claimed them from white families. Since the Freedmen's Bureau defined the youths' legal guardians as their parents or "next of kin," white families harboring black minors separated from their families by the slave trade could expect to encounter freedpeople who were parents, grandparents, aunts or uncles, or even more distantly related kin.

The freedpeople relied on their community networks to locate their children. They also placed notices in metropolitan newspapers and in such public places as community post offices. Freedmen's Bureau agents assisted by sending queries out to their extensive network of offices across the South as well as posting notices in local churches.

The freedpeople did not hesitate to contact Valley Bureau agents and express extreme reluctance in having their children remain in the households of their former owners. The brutalities of slavery had taught them to be wary of white paternalism in any guise. Freedwoman Brown shared with her Frederick County employer her desire to reclaim her grandson Henry from Isaac Williams, a Frederick County farmer. Mrs. Brown noted that Henry's parents had been sold to Williams years before. "[S]he is

---

[5] George Cook to the Winchester Freedmen's Bureau Office, April 21, 1866, Records of the Field Offices for the State of Virginia, BRFAL, 1865-1872, Accession. 44121, Misc. reel 5709, roll 184, frame 763.

particularly desirous that none of them, that is her relatives, shall remain there," her employer told the Bureau.[6] Freedwoman Lucy Jones, who lived in Jefferson County, expressed similar concerns about her grandson. The family who had owned the boy, the Winchester agent explained, "Now holds him in actual slavery." He was "ill treated, badly clothed and unwilling to remain."[7]

The Winchester Bureau's standard communication to white families resisting the freedpeople's efforts to reclaim their children began to have a boiler plate consistency. When Frederick Muse of Frederick County refused to release Freedman Robert Page's four children, the Bureau sent Muse a note: "You refuse to allow him [Page] to take them away, which he has a right to do. You will allow them to go with their father and take with them such personal property as may belong to them."[8]

Because slavery was so unevenly distributed in the Shenandoah Valley and because the Valley had one of Virginia's largest enclaves of Union sympathizers in the pre-Civil War period, whites in the Valley posed no massive resistance to the freedpeople's efforts to claim their children. In Shenandoah County where African Americans accounted for only 6% of the county's population in 1860, George Happ, a Unionist and veteran of the War of 1812, considered his willingness to acknowledge his former bondspeople's right to leave his farm a badge of honor. He fired off a note to the Winchester Bureau rebuking any claim to them: "I have complied with every proclamation I should by President Lincoln." Happ did admit that he continued providing a home for "blind old Larrie and [her] children" on his farm. But far from desiring to retain his former slaves, Happ insisted "No man is more disposed to carry out the Emancipation Proclamation than I am."[9]

---

[6] J. L. Baker to Winchester Freedmen's Bureau, April 23, 1866, Records of the Field Offices for the State of Virginia, BRFAL, 1865-1872, Accession. 44121, Misc. reel 5716, roll 191, frames 791-2.
[7] Captain E. H. Ripley to Captain T.A. McDonnell, May 31, 1868, Records of the Field Offices for the State of Virginia, BRFAL, 1865-1872, Accession. 44121, Misc. reel 5707, roll 182.
[8] Captain McKenzie to Robert Muse, August 31, 1865, Records of the Field Offices for the State of Virginia, BRFAL, 1865-1872, Accession. 44121, Misc. reel 5716, roll 191, frame 115.
[9] George Happ to the Winchester Freedmen's Bureau Office, August 14, 1865, Records of the Field Offices for the State of Virginia, BRFAL, 1865-1872, Accession. 44121, Misc. reel 5716, roll 191, frame 496. Unionists in the Valley like George Happ may have held anti-slavery sentiments or, as conditional Unionists, may have wanted to save the Union, but preserve slavery. The majority of Virginia Unionists lived west of the Blue Ridge Mountains where commercial ties with Pennsylvania and Ohio and such mid-Atlantic

Regardless of their political allegiance, however, former slave owners' paternalistic concern tended to obscure distinctions between their caretaker motives and their desire to retain black minors as a valuable source of exploitable labor. After Freedman William Falls had inquired about his boys at the Winchester Bureau, Bureau agents found them living on the southern Shenandoah Valley farm of their former owner, Mrs. Cassandra McPoole. She reported to the Bureau: "The two children of Wm. Falls spoken of are still with me. They know they are free and can go when they choose. I have often told them so. They, as well as three others I have, prefer to stay with us and I am willing to keep them so long as they see proper to stay, not so much for their services, as from the fact that they have been raised in the family. I feel it a duty to care for them."[10] Yet, in providing a home for William Falls' sons Mrs. McPoole knew that, whatever her benevolent motives, she would have had at her disposal increasingly productive farm workers without having to pay their father for the boys' labor. Nor would she have had to comply with formal apprenticeship provisions.

In seeking the Freedmen's Bureau's help in claiming their children from white households, the freedpeople had to make a case for providing them with a good home. They understood that the agents' commitment to protecting their guardianship rights could yield to economic considerations if necessity dictated. Shortly after the Civil War ended, a Bureau agent allowed a

---

cities as Alexandria and Baltimore prevailed. Slavery was also less prevalent west of the Blue Ridge Mountains than in Tidewater and Piedmont Virginia, although slaveholding too presents a complex picture in the Shenandoah Valley. For example, the 1860 federal census shows that in Clarke County the enslaved population (3,375) approached that of the white population (3,707) with free blacks constituting a small minority (64). In Frederick County, the white population (13,970) significantly outnumbered the enslaved population (2,259) while a substantial free black population (1,208) had grown through natural increase. By contrast, in Shenandoah County the white population (12,827) significantly outnumbered both the enslaved population (1,753) and the free black population (316), Federal Census United States Bureau of the Census (1870). Population Schedule for Clarke, Frederick and Shenandoah counties. Furthermore, in the northern Valley religious sentiments, such as those of pacifist, anti-slavery Quakers, were a factor in determining Union loyalty. See also Brendan Wolfe, "Unionism in Virginia during the Civil War," accessed August 21, 2019, https://www.encyclopediavirginia.org/Unionism_in_Virginia_During_the_Civil_War

[10] Mrs. Cassandra McPoole to Captain McKenzie, December 4, 1865, Records of the Field Offices for the State of Virginia, BRFAL, 1865-1872, Accession. 44121, Misc. reel 5716, roll 191, frame 683.

Frederick County family to keep the girl Sophia Grant, who served as a nurse to the family's children. When her financially struggling single sister tried to claim Sophia, Sophia's mistress, Mrs. Edward Grady, convinced Bureau agents that Sophia was a "sickly girl" who was "violently opposed" to going with her sister. Mrs. Grady had only to raise the specter of Sophia's vulnerability to homelessness and poverty to keep her rather than "send[ing] her out upon the world with no one to take care of her when she could not support herself."[11]

The freedpeople's working class status at times placed them on a middle ground. On the one hand they strove to prevent whites' unfettered access to their children's labor; on the other, the freedpeople at times needed the income supplement placing their children in the white labor market supplied. To retain some control over their children's labor the freedpeople entered into informal, short term work arrangements with white employers that were not legally binding. The freedpeople preferred these informal arrangements to apprenticing their children for many of the same reasons they preferred informal arrangements for their own labor. They had greater flexibility in offering their children's labor on a short term basis. Moreover, when whites mistreated their children or otherwise breached work arrangements, black guardians could more easily withdraw their children from them.

These informal arrangements usually included the employer's provision of room and board, a wage payable to the minor's parents or guardians and, at times, a clothing supplement. Nevertheless, white employers could at times frustrate the entire goal of such arrangements. Freedwoman Easter Strange complained that, while she had sent her son to work for William B. Lowers until Christmas so that he might return with a suit of clothes, Lowers sent him home without any suitable clothing at all.[12]

The freedpeople also complained frequently of their children's mistreatment by white employers. Freedwoman Nancy Lee complained to the Winchester bureau that Charles Burley's widow was "beating and ill treating him [her son] in an unmerciful

---

[11] Mrs. Grady to Winchester Freedmen's Bureau Office, Records of the Field Offices for the State of Virginia, BRFAL, 1865-1872, Accession. 44121, Misc. reel 5716, roll 191, frames 832-33
[12] Captain Chandler's December 27, 1866 communication to William B. Lowers concerning Easter Strange's son. Records of the Field Offices for the State of Virginia, BRFAL, 1865-1872, Accession. 44121, Misc. reel 5715, roll 190, frame 782.

manner."[13] Responding to these complaints, the Virginia legislature in 1867 required that informal labor arrangements meet the same disciplinary requirements as those stipulated by the apprenticeship code; a white employer's "unnecessary or excessive correction" of a black minor qualified as a breach of a work arrangement.[14]

By controlling white employers' access to their children's labor the freedpeople could better shield them from mistreatment and exploitative work. But black youths were also vulnerable to exploitation by elders of their own race. Albert Townley, an elderly black man residing in Warren County, forthrightly told a Bureau agent he wanted to claim his five children from white households in order to bolster his financial security in old age: "I want to get them so I can have the good of them, and I think I ought to have the benefit of them [as hired wage workers] as I am getting old."[15]

Other African American youths found themselves at the mercy of black traffickers. Freedwoman Anna Jones profited from hiring out the children of Henry Strange, a Winchester freedman who had moved to Charlottesville. Since Strange did not want to reunite with his children, the Winchester Bureau planned to find homes for them as Mrs. Jones "appears to have done but little of anything for them."[16]

African American children claimed by single mothers experienced another kind of hardship: living in a household fraught with economic insecurity. While Bureau agents considered the male-headed household the desirable model for establishing the black family's economic self-sufficiency, General Howard acknowledged that Virginia's post-emancipation demographics challenged this model: "[T]housands and thousands [of newly emancipated bondspeople] were poor women with families of children, without husbands to care for them. In Virginia, where large numbers of children were reared to be sold and work further south, there is naturally a large surplus [of single black mothers]."[17]

---

[13] Captain Chandler to Widow Burley, July 15, 1867, Records of the Field Offices for the State of Virginia, BRFAL, 1865-1872, Accession. 44121, Misc. reel 5715, roll 190, frame 823.
[14] *Code of Virginia* (1873) chap. 122: 927.
[15] Alfred Townley to General Alfred Torbert, September 28, 1865, Records of the Field Offices for the State of Virginia, BRFAL, 1865-1872, Accession. 44121, Misc. reel 5716, roll 191, frame 557.
[16] Captain McDonnell to Orlando Brown, March 6, 1868, Records of the Field Offices for the State of Virginia, BRFAL, 1865-1872, Accession. 44121, Misc. reel 5712, roll 187, frame 267.
[17] Howard, *Autobiography*, 2: 42-43.

With only low wage jobs available to them, struggling single mothers faced the always looming threat of having their children taken from them by a local magistrate or overseer of the poor and placed in an apprenticeship. Or, alternatively, Bureau agents could send their children to the black orphanage in Washington, D. C. As they contacted Freedmen's Bureau agents for assistance in keeping their children with them, black women were asserting their new standing as citizens who expected the federal government to advocate for them. Bureau agents did help freedwomen locate jobs. As a temporary measure, if destitute single mothers had no relatives or neighbors to take them in, agents sent them with their children to their county poorhouse until they could find a job. They took care to see that struggling single mothers received rations beyond the Virginia Bureau's official cutoff date for distributing them. Bureau agents also coordinated the receipt of clothing for the women's children from northern and mid-western benevolent organizations.[18]

Tenacious and resourceful in their efforts to keep their children in their care, single mothers independently devised a number of strategies for retaining guardianship of their children. They moved to cities that offered better job prospects. A freedwoman contacted the Bureau from New York City, requesting travel funds to have her daughter reunited with her there. The Winchester Bureau received a request from a destitute widow who wanted her two children sent to her sister in Southbury, Connecticut. A hardworking mother requested her daughter's return from the black orphanage in Washington, asserting she could prove herself competent to support her. "She is now able and willing to take care of her [daughter] and guarantees she will be no further burden to the Govt.," a Winchester agent reported.[19]

---

[18] Michigan Freedmen's Society, Records of the Field Offices for the State of Virginia, BRFAL,1865-1872, Accession. 44121, Misc. reel 5709, roll 184, and Harper's Ferry Freedmen's Bureau Office requesting clothing for women and children from a Freedmen's Aid Society, December 14, 1866, Records of the Field Offices for the State of Virginia, BRFAL,1865-1872, Accession. 44121, Misc. reel 5710, roll 185, frame 190.

[19] Mother's communication to Winchester Freedmen's Bureau Office from New York City in December 1866, Records of the Field Offices for the State of Virginia, BRFAL,1865-1872, Accession. 44121, Misc. reel 6716, roll 191, frame 204; Captain McDonnell to Orlando Brown, December 11, 1867. Records of the Field Offices for the State of Virginia, BRFAL,1865-1872, Accession. 44121, Misc. reel 5707, roll 182; Captain Chandler to Captain McDonnell, October 1, 1867, Records of the Field Offices for the State of Virginia, BRFAL,1865-1872, Accession. 44121, Misc. reel 5715, roll 190, frame 850.

Black youths' prospects for contributing to their families' household economies as wage earners improved as they matured. The majority of black youths participating in the labor force in Clarke and Frederick counties, for example, was between the ages of sixteen and twenty according to the 1870 census. Subjected to the demands of the Valley's post-emancipation labor market, black youths, depending on their age, could therefore be either excluded or valued as wage earners by white employers. Two young orphans, George and Anna Washington, aged three and five, were sent to the Washington orphanage after Winchester Bureau agents searched in vain for a family to take them in. "I have endeavored to put them out but people will not take them on account of their age," an agent reported.[20] When Freedman Isaac Thompson filed suit against Clarke County farmer Edward McCormack for failing to pay Thompson's thirteen-year-old son the wages the two men had agreed on, McCormack told the Freedmen's Bureau Court that he had dismissed the boy shortly after he had begun working for him. McCormack claimed the boy was not "strong enough [to do] the work of a farm."[21]

At times the fate of young black children with little labor market value hung precariously on the thread of a white employer's good will. As the Christmas holiday approached in December of 1866, Winchester businessman L. T. Moore sent nine-year-old John Parker to the Bureau with a note: "I have not much for him to do. Nothing but running errands. I am going to give him some old cloths to keep him warm... It is wrong the child should be left to perish. If you can do better for him than I propose please take him. If not I will save him till spring without he misbehaves."[22] The agent related to Mr. Moore that the Winchester Bureau could do no better by the boy.

Black youths were especially vulnerable to elite planters' shedding of their obligation to continue caring for black members

---

[20] Captain Chandler to General Schofield, September 3, 1866, Records of the Field Offices for the State of Virginia, BRFAL, 1865-1872, Accession. 44121, Misc. reel 5715, roll 190, frame 771.

[21] *Isaac Thompson v. Edward McCormack* tried in the Winchester Freedmen's Bureau Court on December 26, 1865, Records of the Field Offices for the State of Virginia, BRFAL, 1865-1872, Accession. 44121, Misc. reel 5716, roll 191, frame 37.

[22] December 19, 1867, communication to the Winchester Freedmen's Bureau Office. Records of the Field Offices for the State of Virginia, BRFAL, 1865-1872, Accession. 44121, Misc. reel 5711, roll 186, frames 231-2.

of their "white and black family" who had little labor value. Before the Civil War, planters like George Burwell of Clarke County could not send members of their enslaved community off to a county poorhouse if they were of negligible labor value to them. Shortly after the Civil War's end, however, Burwell took full advantage of the option presented to him by slavery's abolition to divest himself of his unprofitable former property. Burwell contacted the Freedmen's Bureau notifying the agents that "I have a family of servants I should be pleased to have you send a wagon and take away." Impervious to the anguish this family would experience by yet another arbitrary separation, Burwell was willing to keep only one of the family's five children.[23]

Black minors faced the prospect of being placed in an apprenticeship if they had no guardians to care for them or had indigent guardians unable to provide for them. Assessing the situation of a young boy residing with his mother in the Frederick County Poorhouse, Captain T.A. McDonnell of the Winchester Bureau related to the Overseer of the Poor that, since his labor was of little value, the boy would have to be apprenticed until he reached adulthood. "Farmers and others do not care to take children of his age, when their services are comparatively useless unless they are bound to them. So that it is impossible to place him in a house, which he can leave at any time."[24]

During Reconstruction a significant readjustment in the apprenticing of black minors did occur, however, as Freedmen's Bureau agents assumed oversight of black minors' apprenticeships. As contract mediators, Bureau agents made sure apprenticeship agreements were voluntary; whites could not compel black parents or guardians to sign contracts under duress. When orphaned youths were bound out, their apprenticeships could be canceled if their parents or guardians later located and claimed them.

Although Virginia's revised post-Civil War black apprenticeship code was much less harsh than those of such southern states as Mississippi and South Carolina, Virginia's code

---

[23] George Burwell to the Winchester Freedmen's Bureau Office, August 21, 1865, Records of the Field Offices for the State of Virginia, BRFAL, 1865-1872, Accession 44121, Misc. Reel 5716, roll 191, frame 489.
[24] Winchester Freedmen's Bureau Office to W. G. Russell (Overseer of the Poor), July 28, 1868, Frederick County, Records of the Field Offices for the State of Virginia, BRFAL, 1865-1872, Accession. 44121, Misc. reel 5708, roll 183.

benefited white "masters" more than it protected black youths.[25] Under the apprenticeship code, masters had the benefit of a black youth's labor until they reached maturity (eighteen for females and twenty-one for males). The code also severely restricted an apprentice's mobility in stipulating that the apprentice "shall not be absent from said master's service day or night without leave." While an apprentice's mistreatment could be appealed to a local magistrate or judge, apprentices who took matters into their own hands and ran away were subject to a penalty as were those who harbored them. Apprentices also had to adhere to a confidentiality oath that, in effect, muffled disapproval of a master's misconduct.

Since apprentices were bound out until they reached legal adulthood, employers were more than compensated by having at their disposal an inexpensive, maturing labor force.[26] In addition to being undercompensated, apprentices were not being trained in work that could significantly enhance their prospects on the labor market once they were released from their contracts. The Freedmen's Bureau agents apprenticed black females to learn the "art and trade of house servant" and black males, to learn the "business of farmhand." Well-intentioned whites did infrequently offer better apprenticeship arrangements. S. D. Buck of Middletown contacted the Winchester Bureau in order to arrange an apprenticeship for a boy formerly owned by Buck's mother. Because the boy's mother was "not capable to raise him as she should " Buck wanted the boy bound out to a Mr. Delanger, a carriage maker, who "will give this boy a good understanding of business if allowed to keep him."[27]

---

[25] *Code of Virginia* (1873), chap. 122: 925-928. The Virginia apprenticeship code was less harsh than those of other southern states and did not discriminate between black and white minor apprentices. Under the South Carolina code, for example, since magistrates had broad discretion in determining whether black minors should be placed in a compulsory apprenticeship, they were at liberty to bind out black youths without their guardians' consent. See the South Carolina apprenticeship code compiled in Walter Fleming, ed., *Documents Relating to Reconstruction* (Morgantown, WV: N.P., 1904), 18-19.

[26] The Freedmen's Bureau indenture records show that the top annual pay for a black female in the fourth year of her apprenticeship was $25. Two orphaned black males bound in apprenticeships, one for four years and one for six years, were both to receive a lump sum payment of $100 and clothing when they fulfilled their contracts at age twenty-one. See Contracts and Indentures, 1865-1868, Records of the Field Offices for the State of Virginia BRFAL, 1865-1872, Accession 44121, Misc. Reel 5717, roll 192.

[27] S. D. Buck to the Winchester Freedmen's Bureau Office, December 21, 1865, Records of the Field Offices for the State of Virginia, BRFAL, 1865-1872, Accession. 44121, Misc. reel 5716, roll 191.

On the other hand, the code did not discriminate between white and black apprentices. Black apprentices had to be offered the same rudiments of literacy as were offered to white apprentices. Masters also had to provide clothing, lodging, and medical care for their apprentices. Moreover, the apprenticeship system prohibited one of slavery's more onerous practices. It prevented apprentices from being commoditized. In the event of the master's death, the apprentice could not be passed on to another designated master nor could apprenticeships be used to pay off the deceased master's debts or other obligations.

Recognizing black youth labor value increased with age, the Virginia legislature also included a provision in the apprenticeship code that afforded black youths an alternative to a long-term apprenticeship. Black males could make their own labor contracts when they reached age fourteen and females, when they reached age twelve. The Winchester Bureau therefore encouraged black youths to make their own labor arrangements as they crossed the legal threshold for doing so. In this way they could avoid compulsory apprenticeships that straight jacketed them in exploitative work until they reached legal adulthood.

Black youths not bound in apprenticeships were, in fact, securing wage labor in the Valley's resilient agricultural economy. In addition to the more extended work arrangements their guardians made for them or that they made for themselves, they had the option of more short-term work arrangements.[28] In a diversified, cyclical farm economy with daily chores punctuated by periods of intensive farm work, Valley farmers and merchant millers were hiring black youths to work for them on an as needed basis. In 1870, Frederick County farmer Kitty Kemper hired James King, an African American youth, for four to five day periods at $0.35 a day. Between 1867 and 1869 Charles Colfelt, a Frederick County merchant miller, hired "col'd boys" during the summer and fall months when his mill was busy processing wheat and corn.

---

[28] For example, in Clarke County six black minors under the age of ten worked, 251 between the ages of ten and fifteen and 348 between the ages of sixteen and twenty. In Frederick County, where family farms had been less dependent on the labor of enslaved African Americans, one minor under the age of ten worked, 129 between the ages of ten and fifteen and 240 between the ages of sixteen and twenty. Calculated from the 1870 federal population census information for Frederick and Clarke counties.

Colfelt also hired a man and his son to "cut corn."²⁹

African American girls, who were in demand as domestics, benefited most from their right to make their own work arrangements once they reached twelve years of age. With reliable domestic workers in demand as black women with families withdrew from white households and turned their attention to their own families, unattached girls with a streak of independence were making favorable work arrangements with their employers. When freedwoman Emily Parker contacted Bureau officials in Winchester seeking word of her daughter Anna, both Bureau agents and Mrs. Parker must have considered Anna's arrangement with the Triplett family an equitable one since they did not disturb it. In his letter to the Bureau, Leven Triplett informed Mrs. Parker that Anna was "perfectly satisfied to remain with us for the usual amount of clothing and pay"³⁰ A young domestic serving in the household of a Mrs. Timberlake in Winchester reported she was getting "pay whenever she want[ed] it" and used her wages to buy clothes. She had no desire to reunite with her mother.³¹

As overseers of black minors' apprenticeships, Bureau agents had also the demanding task of mediating the freedpeople's claims to children bound out without their consent or bound out to masters who mistreated them. The Bureau's red tape, the slowness of communications circulating among Bureau agents and other parties to contested apprenticeships, as well as white employers' unfamiliarity with the Bureau's apprenticeship policy, could delay eager parents' efforts to be reunited with their children.

But those considerations did not deter freedwoman Margaret Webb who operated a boardinghouse in the Winchester area. She showed considerable pluck as she fought to cancel her sons' apprenticeships. Mrs. Webb had not yet reconnected with her sons when the Bureau apprenticed them as orphans to Adolphus White, a farmer in the Lexington area. With no knowledge of the

---

[29] Kitty Kemper Memorandum Book, 1845-1897, Laborers' Accounts and Daybook of Charles Colfelt at Springdale Grist Mills, Frederick County, June 11, 1868-March 1869. Special Collections, Swem Library, College of William & Mary, Williamsburg, VA.
[30] Contracts and Indentures, 1865-1867, BRFAL, 1865-1872, Accession. 44121, Misc. reel 5717, roll 192.
[31] Records of the Field Offices for the State of Virginia, BRFAL, 1865-1872, Accession. 44121, Misc. reel 5716, roll 19, frame 189.

Bureau's policy regarding apprenticeship contracts, White considered his contract legitimate and at first resisted returning the boys to their mother. He later relented as he became more familiar with Bureau policy invalidating contracts made without parental consent. "Mr. White informed me that the boys are at liberty to go whenever called for," the Lexington agent reported. But after a year of dealing with the Bureau's red tape, Margaret Webb took matters into her own hands. She traveled to Lexington and reclaimed her boys from the White family. Describing Mrs. Webb's rescue mission, the Lexington agent noted that when he had instructed White to release the boys, "he told me that they were no longer with him having been taken away by their Mother who I presume could not see the beauty or utility in the Law's delay."[32]

Not all white employers were as compliant as Adolphus White. J. R. Grigsby of Clarke County stridently contested Freedwoman Betsy Brown's efforts to cancel her sons' apprenticeships. She had returned to the Valley from Mississippi and had secured a position with the Grigsby family as a nurse. Grigsby, who had sent her boys to his father's Lexington farm, never produced the apprenticeship contracts. With no evidence he also maligned her character, accusing Betsy of poisoning one of his children. The Bureau was unmoved by Grigsby's tactics and ordered Betsy Brown's children returned to her.[33]

Bureau agents in the Valley were as vigilant in investigating abusive treatment of apprentices as they were in ensuring the consensual nature of apprenticeship contracts. In investigating the case of Betty, an apprenticed domestic servant, Bureau agents were clearly out to demonstrate a new day had arrived in curbing the more persistent brutalities vulnerable young black females had long endured. Betty had run away twice from the Whites, a couple living in the Staunton vicinity. Each time she ran away, Betty had found refuge with the Rhodes family.

Sending a third party, a Mr. Watts, to retrieve the girl after

---

[32] The Margaret Webb case, Records of the Field Offices for the State of Virginia, BRFAL, 1865-1872, Accession. 44121, Misc. reel 5715, roll 190, frames 768, 270, 813 and Misc. reel 5716, roll 191, frames 180-181.

[33] Captain Chandler to Mrs. J. R. Grigsby, June 19, 1866, Records of the Field Offices for the State of Virginia, BRFAL, 1865-1872, Accession. 44121, Misc. reel 5716, roll 191. The Betsy Brown case is referenced in: Records of the Field Offices for the State of Virginia, BRFAL, 1865-1872, Accession. 44121, Misc. reel 5715, roll 190, frames 752, 765, 766 and Misc. roll 5716, roll 191, frames 167, 177.

she ran away again from the Whites, White accused Rhodes of harboring her illegally. White put pressure on Rhodes to release her lest he be forced to pay the penalty for illegally harboring a bound servant. "I am surprised at your conduct in regard to her knowing as you do that she is bound to me. I will sue the law as regards apprentices being harbored knowingly," White threatened.[34]

Rattled by this accusation, Rhodes sent White a note making clear he had no intention of harboring Betty. Even though he knew the Whites had mistreated her, Rhodes apologetically related to White: "Sir, Your girl Betty (colored) is at my place and if you want her please come or send after her as I don't want to keep her if you have an agreement with her. Mr. Thomas Watts called for her and took her part way and tied her to a post and she got loose and ran away. You must not think that I want to keep her from you as such is not the case."[35]

Although Rhodes may have been aware of the law's provision protecting apprentices from mistreatment, he decided the more important provision was that penalizing those who harbored runaways. The Bureau, by contrast, focused its investigation on the victim Betty, interviewing her privately to obtain her testimony without pressure from either the Whites or Rhodes. Betty reported that Mr. and Mrs. White whipped her "severely." With six male witnesses present, Betty stated that she wanted to live with the Rhodes family. Although the outcome of the case does not appear in the Bureau's records, it is probable that Betty was released from her abusive situation and allowed to go live with the Rhodes family. In another documented case the Bureau required a master to release a boy from his contract and to stand trial for the boy's charge of being ill-treated. The boy subsequently returned to his former master in Staunton.

As an increasing number of freedpeople found employment and were able to support their children, they redoubled their efforts

---

[34] Case regarding apprentice Betty's mistreatment by the White family. Records of the Field Offices for the State of Virginia, BRFAL, 1865-1872, Accession. 44121, Misc. reel 5715, roll 190, frame 670. Entire case, frames 670-673.

[35] Mr. W. Rhodes to Mr. G. A. White, October 19, 1868, Augusta County Records of the Field Offices for the State of Virginia, BRFAL, 1865-1872, Accession. 44121, Misc. reel 5715, roll 190, frame 673.

to locate them after sometimes arduous searches. Freedman William Kenney, a Lexington boot maker and repairer, approached the Lexington Bureau seeking custody of his son William. William had been bound out to a Mr. White, a Rockbridge County man, who had passed William along to his brother in New Town. The Lexington agent was favorably impressed by the witnesses Kenney marshaled to defend his reputation as a good parent and provider. "The witnesses," the agent reported, "give me assurance that the parents are abundantly able to take care of the boy and give him all the advantages of the Freedmen's school in Lexington."[36] Since Kenney's other sons had been "sold away to persons and parts unknown to him," Kenney must have considered reclaiming his son the bittersweet fruit of the Valley's emerging post-emancipation social order. Kenney's family embodied African Americans' aspirations for a life in freedom: living together as a family, enjoying economic self-sufficiency by their own labor and able to offer their child a better future by educating him.

The Bureau's indenture records for the Shenandoah Valley show that the agents mediated only ten apprenticeship contracts between 1865 and 1869, the period during which the Virginia Bureau maintained offices in the Valley. These records underscore the agents' success in preventing the apprenticeship system from becoming a legal mechanism for re-enslaving orphaned and indigent black youths.[37] The apprentices were all orphans between the ages of twelve and sixteen. With black females in demand as domestic workers, all but two of the apprenticeships were made for black males. In post-Reconstruction Frederick County, only one apprenticeship contract was arranged for a black girl, Roberta Chismore, a contract that effectively concluded the County's black apprenticeship system in 1871.[38]

Several factors contributed to the decline of the apprenticeship system in the post-emancipation Shenandoah Valley. The Freedmen's Bureau agents' vigilant supervision of the contracts likely had a chilling effect on white employers. In the

---

[36] William Kenney case of January 1866. Records of the Field Offices for the State of Virginia, BRFAL, 1865-1872, Accession. 44121, Misc. reel 5715, roll 190, frame 665.
[37] See Indentures 1865-1872, Records of the Field Offices for the State of Virginia, BRFAL, 1865-1872, Accession. 44121, Misc. reel 5717, roll 192, frames 144-173.
[38] Frederick County Free Negro Papers, 1798-1871, 4/F/32/1/2/, Box 12, "Emancipation Papers, Indentures," Library of Virginia, Richmond, VA.

Valley's resilient postwar agricultural economy, with its flexible labor market, parents and guardians could avoid apprenticing their children by placing them in short term work arrangements. Moreover, as they arrived at the legal age to do so, black youths could negotiate their own labor arrangements. Other youths were included in their parents' labor contracts. Clarke County farmer W. H. Barton, for example, included his tenant David Lovett's son in Lovett's work contract. As an incentive to Lovett, Barton provided for the boy's clothing and medical care in exchange for his performing general farm work.[39]

The most significant factor, however, in keeping black youths from being bound out in apprenticeships was the social safety net provided by both black and white households. With no black orphanages in Virginia before the Quakers established theirs in 1871, and with only one over-burdened black orphanage in Washington, D.C., serving the larger region, Bureau agents had to follow General Howard's lead in respecting traditional social safety networks within each Valley community.[40] Inter-generational black households in Clarke County, for example, provided homes for up to eighty-one black youths other than those belonging to the household's nuclear family and up to ninety such youths were living in Frederick County's inter-generational black households. In both counties, black youths in white households were more likely to be listed as laborers in the 1870 census. Some of these youths were placed in white households to fulfill work arrangements the freedpeople made with white families. Others, out of necessity,

---

[39] Freedmen's labor contracts mediated by the Winchester Freedmen's Bureau, October 1865 - March 1866, Records of the Field Offices for the State of Virginia, BRFAL, 1865-1872, Accession. 44121, Misc. reel 5717, roll 192, frames 99-129.
[40] General Howard observed, "[T]he colored people themselves of this city [New Orleans] have largely cared for the orphans of their friends and acquaintances in their own families and thus when orphanage was at its height, generously saved the government of much expense." Howard, *Autobiography*, 2: 262. Historian Ira Berlin and his colleagues note that African Americans "understood their society in the idiom of kinship." This "kinship expressed a broad range of mutual obligation." See Berlin, et al. In "Afro-American Families in the Transition from Slavery to Freedom," *Radical History Review*, 42 (Fall 1988): 89. Historian Jacqueline Jones notes that "these [black kinship] obligations assumed greater significance in nineteenth-century African-American life than in immigrant or poor white communities because blacks possessed a distinctive low economic status, a condition that denied them the advantages of an extensive associational life beyond the kin group and the advantages and disadvantages resulting from mobility opportunities." See Jacqueline Jones, *Labor of Love, Labor of Sorrow: Black Women, Work and the Family, from Slavery to the Present* (New York: Vintage Books, 1986), 45.

remained in the households of their former owners.⁴¹

What orphaned black youths in the Valley had if they remained with their former owners was shelter, food, and the security of familiar surroundings. William Cross, a retired Clarke County farmer, related that his grandfather, William W. Cross, was only nine when the Civil War ended. As an orphaned minor, William W. Cross had few other options than to remain in his master's household. Cross "probably didn't know his parents," his grandson related. "He might have known his mother. The landowner was his daddy. He wasn't sold. His brothers was sold. He was all by himself when emancipated. They kept him on. He didn't have no reason to leave. That was his home. Couldn't have went nowhere. Didn't have nowhere to go. If he'd went somewhere, someone would have to take him in and feed him."⁴² William W. Cross became a tenant farmer in post-emancipation Clarke County, and his son, William Cross' father, became one of the County's earliest black landowners.

Unbeknownst to him Thomas Nelson, a former Confederate officer, planter, and editor of the *Clarke County Courier,* paid the freedpeople a compliment when he observed during the Valley's final year of Reconstruction that "the [black] boys and girls are mostly brought up without any regular employment and lead an exceedingly idle life."⁴³ Former slave owners like Nelson had considered such "idle" youths a social menace to be placed under the authority of whites as soon as possible. A month after the Civil War's close the *Richmond Times* observed that "the number of Negro boys who are to be seen on the streets idle and often vicious shows that the apprenticeship system cannot be too soon adopted."⁴⁴

As freedpeople in the post-emancipation Shenandoah Valley strove to reunite their families and protect their children from whites' labor exploitation they were asserting a parental

---

⁴¹ For example, by 1870 black minors in Clarke County's labor force totaled 575 and in Frederick County, 379. In Clarke County 52% of minors in black households worked, while 91% of those in white households did. In Frederick County, 31% of black minors in black households worked while 53% of those in white households did. Calculated from the 1870 federal population census for Clarke and Frederick counties.
⁴² William Cross, interview by author, African American Episcopal Church Parish Hall, Berryville, VA, July 28, 2006.
⁴³ *The Clarke County Courier,* April 9, 1869.
⁴⁴ *Richmond Times,* May 12, 1865

guardianship right fundamental to grounding their lives in freedom. But their household finances at times required the freedpeople to make labor arrangements with whites for their children's labor. With the assistance of Valley Bureau agents their efforts to deny whites unfettered access to their children's labor were successful to the extent that work arrangements freedmen and women made with white employers for their children's labor were consensual. These arrangements could also be canceled if their children were mistreated or employers otherwise breached the terms of the work agreement. For their part, far from being body snatchers, whites were taking advantage of a free labor market to employ black minors only when it was profitable to do so.

While these adjustments to their labor occurred, black youths were subjected to the turbulence of a social order in flux. They experienced both whites' fierce resistance to their kinfolks' guardianship claims and the insecurities of working in a free labor market where they might be let go by white employers at any time. When reunited with their kinfolk, black youths could find themselves living once more within white households as the result of short-term labor arrangements. While some experienced the security of continued care by their former owners, other youths were exploited by traffickers in their labor. Many black youths were eventually reunited with kinfolk who could provide them with a stable home life, but others were vulnerable to state intervention in their living arrangements if their guardians were unable to support them or if they were unclaimed orphans.

Yet, in the midst of turbulent circumstances beyond their control, black youths were also carving out areas of autonomy. Freedmen's Bureau agents encouraged them to make their own work arrangements as they reached the legal age to do so. They also acted on their own emancipation aspirations. In the Civil War's aftermath, Lexington area boys who had been bound out before the Civil War wasted no time in fleeing from their masters, claiming that slavery's abolition had freed them from being bound servants.[45] As Freedmen's Bureau agents cooperated with missionary societies in establishing schools for them, black youths were also embracing

---

[45] Lieutenant Tubbs' to the Winchester Freedmen's Bureau Office, September 23, 1865, Records of the Field Offices for the State of Virginia, BRFAL, 1865-1872, Accession. 44121, Misc. reel 5709, roll 184, frame 336.

educational opportunity as the leaven of freedom. A Winchester agent reported that a boy bound out before the War sought to cancel his apprenticeship "in order that he may have an opportunity to attend school and fit himself for the duties of a free man."[46]

---

[46] Captain McDonnell to Orlando Brown, October 23, 1868, Records of the Field Offices for the State of Virginia, BRFAL, 1865-1872, Accession. 44121, Misc. reel 5712, roll 187, frames 368-9.

"Hardships and Dangers Will Bind Men as Brothers"
The 170th Ohio National Guard in the Summer of 1864

Jon-Erik Gilot

As darkness blanketed the Cool Spring battlefield on the evening of July 18, 1864, the men of the 170th Ohio National Guard might have asked themselves how they arrived at that moment. The majority of the regiment's officers and enlisted men avoided direct involvement in the Civil War for the majority of their enlistment. Just when it appeared their 100-day term of service might leave them safely ensconced in the forts around Washington, D.C., the bottom fell out. Their colonel, Miles Saunders, had quietly resigned his commission seventeen days earlier. Hours later the regiment was ordered to move to Harpers Ferry where for the first time they experienced shots fired in anger. Now they found themselves on the wrong side of the Shenandoah River, the only federal troops left on that side after reinforcements failed to materialize and orders to withdraw did not reach them. While home lay beyond the Confederate troops prowling across the field, safety lay beyond the river at their backs.

"The regiment must be brought up to the minimum standard..."

On April 24, 1864, Ohio Adjutant General Benjamin Cowen issued General Order No. 12, calling all Ohio National Guard infantry in the state into active service for a term of one hundred days.[1] The men were to be uniformed, armed, equipped, transported, paid by the federal government, and operate outside Ohio's borders. Telegraphers, railroad workers, and steamboat

---

[1] *Belmont Chronicle*, April 28, 1864

operators, occupations deemed essential to the war effort in their civilian capacity, were exempted from service. Any other members not reporting at their designated place of rendezvous on May 2, would be classified deserters.

Ohio would join Indiana, Illinois, Iowa, and Wisconsin in enlisting more than 80,000 militia and National Guard troops for a term of one hundred days during the spring and summer of 1864. Their service would consist of guarding railroads, blockhouses, prisons, and forts.

In eastern Ohio, Harrison County merchant Miles J. Saunders, an outspoken Democrat, received orders to consolidate the 74th and 78th battalions Ohio National Guard for muster into federal service with the designation of the 170th Ohio National Guard. Saunders, who served briefly with the 13th Ohio Infantry in the summer of 1861, was commissioned colonel and tasked with leading 850 men from Harrison County and neighboring Belmont County. His command of the regiment would prove tenuous at best.

Situated among the rolling hills of southeastern Ohio, Belmont and Harrison counties were primarily agrarian. Area farmers utilized the Ohio River to ship crops as far south as New Orleans. The *St. Clairsville Gazette* reported that the mobilization of the Ohio National Guard would present a "terrible drain on the agricultural interests" in Belmont County with the calling up of the National Guard.[2] The outbreak of war threatened financial disaster for these counties with business interests more closely aligned to the south and west than the north and east. With a preponderance of Virginia script in circulation, one Belmont resident wrote in the summer of 1861 that "money is spent by the market folks as soon as they get it fearing that it may become worthless on their bonds."[3] Consequently antiwar sentiment remained strong in both counties throughout the war. Abraham Lincoln lost Belmont County by more than 1,200 votes in the 1860 election; McClellan carried the county in 1864. Both county seats were home to strong Democratic newspapers with the *St. Clairsville Gazette* one of the state's most outspoken Copperhead newspapers.

Both counties were likewise home to a significant

---

[2] *St. Clairsville Gazette*, May 5, 1864
[3] Caleb H. Cope to Alexis Cope, June 6, 1861, Cope Family Papers, Historical Society of Mount Pleasant, Ohio. Cited hereafter as HSMP.

population of Quakers. The Quaker Yearly Meeting House in nearby Mount Pleasant, Ohio, annually hosted all Quakers west of the Allegheny Mountains for a week of meetings and prayer. This prompted thousands of Quakers to permanently settle in the area. While some local Quakers chose to shoulder arms during the early years of the conflict, many more espoused the nonviolence tenet of their faith and opted to stay home, enlisting in local National Guard battalions. As such the 170th Ohio (Company G of Belmont County, in particular) likely held more Quaker soldiers, as participants both willing and unwilling, than any other regiment fielded from Ohio during the Civil War.

Captain James G. Henderson, Co. G
(*Courtesy Linda Langmyer private collection*)

The 74th and 78th battalions consolidated at Bellaire, Ohio, on May 2, 1864. Located along the Ohio River near Wheeling, West Virginia, Bellaire had been a launching point for George B. McClellan's 1861 Western Virginia campaign and served as a vital hub during the massive transfer of the Army of the Potomac's XI and XII Corps the previous autumn en route to Chattanooga. The regiment organized at Camp Jefferson, a training camp briefly located at Bellaire in the summer of 1861. After two hours of drill on May 3, Saunders issued all of the men a seven-day furlough to return home.

Perturbed by the limited training, Benjamin Cowen telegraphed Saunders on May 5 with orders more explicit. "[Your] regiment must be brought to the minimum standard...for the speedy organization of the National Guard," urged Cowen.[4] Most of the men arrived back at Bellaire on May 10, where the regiment remained for the next week. The unit officially mustered into Union service on May 13 and 14. On the 15th the 170th received its uniforms. Two days later, without receiving any sufficient amount of training or drill due to near continuous rain, the men boarded steamboats, which carried them across the river to Benwood, West Virginia. There they climbed aboard the cars of the Baltimore & Ohio Railroad and headed east for the seat of war.

"Does the 170th wish to go to the front?"

After an exhausting five days of bridge, track, and mechanical failures, the regiment arrived in Washington, D.C., on May 22. Assigned to the Lieutenant Colonel J.A. Haskins' division, 22nd Corps, the regiment was broken up and transferred to the various batteries and forts located northwest of the city, including Battery Vermont and Forts Gaines, Simmons, Mansfield, Bayard, Sumner, and DeRussy. While the regiment trained twice daily on the forts' heavy artillery armaments, the men also enjoyed leisurely moments highlighted by fishing and visits to the White House and the Smithsonian.

Unfortunately, the health of the regiment declined precipitously at this time. Poor sanitation and crowded living conditions prompted outbreaks of measles. Isaac Cope, a Quaker in Company G bemoaned their living conditions. He wrote that "we find every place we go very dirty and everything out of order."[5] In another letter Cope described swarms of flies that plagued the men, noting "there are more flies out here in one hour than there are in ten years [at home]...and they are as tame as kittens. It is virtually impossible to sleep in the day time unless you have somebody to fend the flies off. One person can't begin to do it – it requires three

---

[4] Benjamin R. Cowan to Miles J. Saunders, May 5, 1864, copy of letter in author's possession.
[5] Isaac G. Cope to Elizabeth Dungan, June 7, 1864, HSMP.

or four."⁶

On June 1, 1864, James B. Crawford, regimental surgeon, implored Colonel Saunders to bring the regiment's medical staff to full strength. "The welfare of your command must imperatively demand the filling up of the medical staff," explained Crawford, who was debilitated by dysentery. "One man is utterly unable for the task of attending to the wants of the regiment."⁷ A letter written on June 27, published in the *Cadiz Republican* several weeks later, noted that while the dysentery that plagued the regiment had by that time subsided, "measles are still prevalent...forty five have had them severely. Mumps are now in camp."⁸ To supplement their rations and improve their diet the men stationed at Fort DeRussy grew a garden of fresh vegetables, while men at Fort Sumner and Battery Vermont ate fish and eels fresh from the Potomac River.

In addition to the health issues which plagued the regiment, the fact that the command was dispersed throughout various fortifications prevented the establishment of regimental cohesion and esprit de corps. On June 5, Isaac Cope penned a letter home that described the regiment's morale:

> Last night...there was a dispatch come to Head Quarters 170ᵗʰ Regt couched in these words – 'Does the 170ᵗʰ wish to go to the front?' You may imagine the excitement these few words raised in camp. The men had to vote upon it and were given 1 hour to make up their minds. There was a great deal of talking done in that hour. A few wished to go but a larger majority wished to stay. The vote was taken and our Co voted 10 to go and 73 to stay. The vote of the whole regiment was 80 to go and the balance wished to stay. What do you think that speaks for the patriotism of the 170ᵗʰ?

> It was a truly knotty question to decide upon whether we would go down before Richmond and assist Grant and the gallant men in his command or whether we would remain where we are. I was never more puzzled in my life to know

---

⁶ Isaac G. Cope to Elizabeth Dungan, June 14, 1864, HSMP.
⁷ James B. Crawford to Miles J. Saunders, June 1, 1864, copy of letter in author's possession.
⁸ *Cadiz Republican,* July 13, 1864.

what would be right for me to do in any case than in this. As far as I was individually concerned I would rather go and act the soldier in earnest and help Grant and his suffering army than to remain where we are playing the soldier but as a member of Co. G I didn't feel as though my vote was my own. If a majority of the company wanted to go the whole company would undoubtedly have to go and there were a great many men who did not wish to go. Men who had left families in Ohio. Men who said that they wouldn't go. That they would die first. Who claimed that they had been swindled into the service. That they never enlisted for the purpose of going to the front or even out of the state. And the question with me was have I a right to say go when by voting go I might send men to the front who would rather do almost anything else."[9]

Cope described a similar vote that occurred in the 163rd Ohio with nearly identical results; however, that regiment was in fact ordered to the front. "Our turn will come next and one of these days up will come an order for the 170th to go," Cope noted. "If we are needed I will say Amen to the order."[10]

Isaac G. Cope, seated at left, served as the 170th's acting assistant surgeon
(*Courtesy Robert Bundy private collection*)

---

[9] Isaac G. Cope to Elizabeth Dungan, June 5 1864, HSMP.
[10] Ibid.

With the departure of the 163rd Ohio, Colonel Haskins gave command of the division's second brigade, of which the 170th was part, to Colonel Saunders—a man who inspired little confidence in the men under his command. He was lackadaisical in consolidating his regiment and chastised by superiors for not understanding how to fill out basic military paperwork. In a letter printed in the *Belmont Chronicle* a member of the 170th praised many of the regiment's commissioned officers by name, but issued no plaudits to Saunders.[11] Subsequent articles and reminiscences of the regiment written by its members in the *Belmont Chronicle, St. Clairsville Gazette, Cadiz Sentinel* and the *National Tribune* failed to mention Saunders.

Haskins, a West Point graduate and career military man who lost an arm in the Mexican-American War, perhaps thought better of placing Saunders at the head of a brigade. Haskins, however, changed his mind, removed Saunders from brigade command, and turned over the brigade to Colonel John Marble, 151st Ohio Infantry. One Harrison County soldier wrote that Saunders could surely have commanded the brigade "had he been as ambitious for power as most military men are."[12] Instead, Saunders took leave from the regiment shortly thereafter and quietly resigned his commission on July 1, 1864. In May 2011, a large cache of wartime letters, documents, and artifacts relating to Colonel Saunders was parceled out and sold on eBay. While I was able to purchase several documents, the ability to tell more fully Saunders' story likely dissipated with the rest.

"Shot & shell plenty..."

With Saunders' departure, Lieutenant Colonel Arthur Higgins assumed temporary command of the regiment. Higgins, a veteran of the Mexican-American War, was by all accounts well-liked and respected by the men of the 170th. He had earlier served as a captain in the 25th Ohio Infantry and had been seriously wounded at the Battle of McDowell in May 1862. He remained in command of the regiment for the next six weeks until the colonelcy was officially filled by Lewis Lewton, captain of Company K on August 15, 1864.

As command responsibilities shifted in the 170th Ohio, the

---

[11] *Belmont Chronicle*, June 2, 1864.
[12] *Cadiz Republican*, July 13, 1864

military situation intensified at Petersburg, Virginia. Facing unrelenting pressure from the Army of the Potomac, Confederate general Robert E. Lee dispatched the army's Second Corps, approximately 14,000 men, under the command of General Jubal A. Early to the Shenandoah Valley in the hope that Early's operations in the region would raise anxieties about Washington's safety among Union war-planners and prompt General Ulysses S. Grant to move troops from Petersburg to either the nation's capital or the Valley to deal with Old Jube. Early routed Union general David Hunter's command at Lynchburg. The Army of Northern Virginia's Second Corps then marched north, down the Valley, prepared to clear the small Union garrisons at both Martinsburg and Harpers Ferry.

With Confederates approaching Harpers Ferry on July 4, Union troops pulled out of Bolivar, Camp Hill, and the lower town of Harpers Ferry, retiring across the Potomac River to Maryland Heights. Joined there by the Martinsburg garrison, General Franz Sigel assumed command of a rag-tag force prepared to blunt Early's river crossing. The Union high command frantically searched the depleted capital defenses for troops to reinforce Sigel's command. The 170th Ohio were among the troops summoned to Sigel's support.

On the morning of July 4, Brigadier General Albion P. Howe, then in command of the artillery depot in Washington, D.C., was ordered to assume command of the 170th Ohio, and along with some dismounted cavalry then at Camp Stoneman, was ordered to aid in the defense of Harpers Ferry. Each man in the regiment received enough rations for three days along with 100 rounds of ammunition. All of the regiment's sick, totaling fifty men, were left at Fort Sumner under the charge of Private Isaac Cope, then acting as assistant surgeon. The regiment proceeded at once to Soldiers' Rest and the following morning boarded a 7:00 a.m. train for Harpers Ferry.

At 3:00 a.m. on July 6, the train reached Sandy Hook. The regiment disembarked and by 6:00 a.m. marched toward Maryland Heights where they were immediately thrown into line of battle. One member of Company A simply remembered the day as "shot and shell plenty."[13] The regiment remained in line of battle until

---

[13] Unidentified Diary, Civil War Times Illustrated Collection, U.S. Army Heritage and

Saturday, July 9. Frustrated, Jubal Early bypassed Maryland Heights the previous day to continue his march east towards Middletown and Frederick. During this time the 170th expended much of its ammunition and managed to capture a few prisoners. Word of the battle on Maryland Heights reached the sick of the regiment still recuperating at Fort Sumner. Isaac Cope wrote that "Dr. Crawford is alone with the Regt and if it gets into a fight and many are wounded they will suffer for want of attention...I would like to be with them on this account."[14] Cope's fears for his regiment would soon be realized.

On July 14, the first of General Hunter's troops arrived at Harpers Ferry. The 170th, having had nearly a week to rest and recuperate after its first battle, was assigned to the First Brigade, First Division in Hunter's Army of West Virginia. Hunter's men were poised to contest the retreat of Early's footsore Confederates, who had tramped all the way to the outskirts of Washington, D.C., before withdrawing to the Shenandoah Valley.

"We soon found... Early's whole force in line waiting for us."

The First Division began its pursuit on July 15, crossing the Potomac River and advancing to Hillsboro, Virginia. Here General George Crook assumed command of the Union advance, assigning Colonel Joseph Thoburn to command the First Division. A physician from Wheeling, Thoburn was the popular commander of the 1st West Virginia Infantry and knew many of the men serving in the 170th. Under Thoburn, Colonel George D. Wells of the 34th Massachusetts commanded the First Brigade. Wells' brigade advanced from Hillsboro on July 16, passing Waterford and arriving at Purcellville late that night after marching twenty miles.

Breaking camp at Purcellville at 4:00 a.m. on July 18, the 170th Ohio and Crook's army marched west to meet Early's troops, who crossed the Shenandoah River at Snickers Gap two days before. Meeting stiff Confederate resistance at Castleman's Ferry, General Horatio G. Wright, having united his Sixth Corps with Crook's command, opted for a crossing two miles downstream at Island Ford. Thoburn's division was directed to cross the river. It reached

---

Education Center, Carlisle, PA.
[14] Isaac G. Cope to Elizabeth Dungan, July 7, 1864, Ken Mitchell private collection.

Island Ford around 3:30 p.m. Private Benjamin Bogardus of the 170th recalled that the Shenandoah River was "about breast-deep and the bottom very slippery."[15] The crossing did not go uncontested as a contingent of troops from the 42nd Virginia Infantry attempted to stymie Thoburn's advance. That effort proved futile.

Once across, Thoburn deployed his command. The 170th Ohio occupied a position on the left of the Union line, guarding the southern approach to Island Ford while the remainder of Thoburn's division crossed the river and filed north on an old road that snaked along the river. The regiment formed into line of battle and threw out skirmishers to probe the Confederates who contested their crossing. The skirmishers reported back that the troops in front were not cavalry or rear guard, but two veteran infantry regiments. Beyond them were two full divisions of Confederate infantry under Generals John B. Gordon and Gabriel C. Wharton, with yet another two divisions beyond them. Private Bogardus recalled that "We soon found, as we thought then and know now, Early's whole force in line waiting for us."[16] With this information Crook ordered Thoburn to call off the flanking movement and instead occupy the area commanding the ford and wait for reinforcements.

Island Ford from the east bank of the Shenandoah River
(Photo by author)

With three Confederate divisions under Gordon, Wharton, and Robert Rodes turning to meet the threat at their rear, the 170th

---

[15] *National Tribune*, February 25, 1892.
[16] Ibid.

and the other regiments of the First Division began to construct light breastworks, utilizing fence rails and fieldstones. As the advancing Confederates deployed into line of battle, troops under Colonel George Patton lined up across the field from Wells' men, driving in the Union skirmishers, but not attempting a general advance. The battle would otherwise unfold on the Union right flank, where Rodes' division threatened to envelop Thoburn's position. To meet the threat Thoburn called on Wells, who moved the 116th and 123rd Ohio from the left of the line to the far right. This movement left the 170th Ohio's left flank in the air with Confederates still lurking south at Castleman's Ford.

As the battle evolved, Rodes' assaults weakened Thoburn's right flank while the center withered under an intense fire from Wharton's division. Reinforcements from General James Ricketts failed to materialize and panic began to set in among some of Thoburn's command, portions of his command fleeing the battlefield less than an hour after it began. However, the determined fighting of Thoburn's men and artillery support from the eastern shore of the river held the Confederates at bay until sunset when Thoburn ordered a withdrawal to the Shenandoah River's eastern shore. The 170th Ohio's John W. Osburn recalled that "the balls were flying thick" as the regiment fell back, some abandoning their arms and equipment on the field.[17] Osburn also noted that three companies of the 170th—B, G, and K—did not receive the order to retreat. These companies instead held their position long into the night.

Known by a variety of names, the Battle of Cool Spring had been a difficult one for the 170th. While they were spared the vicious fighting experienced on Thoburn's right, the regiment had stood under a withering fire throughout the day and three companies were forced to make a dangerous nighttime river crossing. Upon reaching the safety of the eastern shore, the men undoubtedly began to take stock of who was missing. The regimental surgeon, James B. Crawford, opted to stay behind with the wounded and was captured. Sergeant William Gamble likewise remained on the river's western side with the wounded and was captured. He died four months later in a Confederate prison in Danville, Virginia.

---

[17] *National Tribune,* January 21, 1892.

Private Daniel Warner of Company B was carried from the field badly wounded, a ball crushing his arm between the elbow and shoulder and severing an artery; he died one month later.

The casualty numbers for the 170th at Cool Spring include two men killed, nineteen wounded, and two captured. Those numbers however do not take into consideration soldiers such as William Rankin, who became chilled while crossing the river and died of exposure three weeks later, or John Gundy of Company B, who ruptured his groin while crossing the river, the injury resulting in an infection and fever that eventually claimed his life on October 30, 1864.

"The wildest scenes of excitement"

With federal troops moving in from Charles Town and Martinsburg on July 19, Early withdrew his troops west toward Winchester. For the 170th and the rest of Thoburn's division the 19th was a day to recuperate. The next morning the men crossed the river for a third time and revisited the battlefield. Private Bogardus recalled an unsettling scene of finding some corpses being "partly eaten by hogs."[18] At 6:00 a.m. on July 22 the Army of West Virginia departed the battlefield, covering twenty miles and encamping just south of Winchester along Opequon Creek on the Kernstown battlefield of 1862.

The regiment spent the following day constructing "strong fortifications of rails, logs and stones" on the right of the federal line.[19] On July 24, as Early's Confederates turned and began probing the federal position, Wells' brigade advanced its line one half mile. The 170th Ohio deployed skirmishers under the command of Adjutant Edward T. Affleck, a young newspaper editor from Belmont County. As the skirmishers sparred with North Carolinians under Confederate general Stephen D. Ramseur, a brigade of cavalry under Brigadier General William. L. 'Mudwall' Jackson began testing Wells' flank. In doing so Jackson's men cut off a number of skirmishers from the brigade, among them three men of the 170th including Affleck, whose mother had begged him to resign from the Ohio National Guard before being mustered into

---

[18] *National Tribune*, February 25, 1892.
[19] Thomas C. Dungan to Elizabeth Dungan, July 31, 1862, Ken Mitchell private collection.

service. She wrote that "I am heartsick and remain at home to brood over my troubles...my only remaining son is to be taken from me."[20] Affleck spent the next eight months in captivity at Camp Asylum, Salisbury, and at Richmond before being paroled in March 1865.

Edward T. Affleck
(*Courtesy Martins Ferry Area Historical Society*)

The pressure from Jackson's flanking maneuver, coupled with the collapse of the federal left flank, spelled disaster for Crook's outnumbered army. The 170th and two other regiments from Wells' brigade were detailed to cover the army's wagon train as far as Bunker Hill, West Virginia, twelve miles north. Thomas Dungan, a Quaker of Company G recalled:

> *We thought we would stop when we got back to our breastworks but we made straight back to the rear of W[inchester]. The Rebel Cavalry began to harass our rear and created considerable confusion. When we struck the pike the wildest scenes of excitement were going on. Infantry, artillery, cavalry and wagons were mingled in confusion which is perfectly indescribable. Horses*

---

[20] Mary Affleck to Sarah Forrer, September 20, 1863, Forrer-Peirce-Wood Collection, Dayton Metro Library, Dayton, OH.

were run down, wagons smashed, artillery abandoned and thousands of dollars of government stores burned."[21]

Thomas C. Dungan
(*Courtesy Debbie Lund private collection*)

The 170th performed ably during the retreat, even helping to pull the guns of Battery F, 1st West Virginia Light Artillery from the road near Stephenson's Depot and then wheeling them by hand back to Bunker Hill. Arriving at Bunker Hill around 10:00 p.m. the men rested for approximately four hours before continuing the retreat towards Martinsburg. Water was scarce during the retreat. Thomas Dungan recalled that "we just drank what we could get. We would sip it up when it was so muddy that it would hardly run and drink it down and called it good."[22] The skies opened early on the morning of July 25, drenching the footsore soldiers. Dungan further recalled that "I never saw such walking before. Where Sunday the dust was four or five inches deep now the mud was much deeper. The road being trampled by thousands of horses and men you may imagine what it must have been."[23] Another member of the 170th related that "The retreat from Winchester to Bunker Hill...is

---

[21] Thomas C. Dungan to Elizabeth Dungan, July 31, 1862, Ken Mitchell private collection.
[22] Ibid.
[23] Ibid.

indelibly fixed in the minds of all 'our boys.'"[24]

"Worn out, weary, and footsore"

The retreat continued to Martinsburg, the 170th arriving by 11:00 a.m. on July 25. With Confederate cavalry under the command of Brigadier General John C. Vaughn in the area, the 170th deployed to meet the threat and allow time for the Union wagon train to continue its retreat. Sharp skirmishing with Vaughn's horsemen cost the regiment an additional seven casualties.

The regiment followed the wagon train that evening. It reached opposite Williamsport, Maryland, early the next morning. There they crossed the Potomac River into Maryland and advanced to Boonsboro, and then to Sharpsburg, where they camped for the night. The 170th Ohio continued their march on July 27, reaching Sandy Hook. When they reached Sandy Hook they were pleasantly surprised to find Isaac Cope and a number of the men who had taken ill at Fort Sumner in Washington, D.C. The Buckeyes also visited several of those wounded at Cool Spring. Contemplating all the regiment had passed through since it left the nation's capital, Thomas Dungan noted that "Such congratulations as were passed are not often witnessed. Hardships and dangers will bind men as brothers."[25]

The next day the regiment was ordered to Halltown, West Virginia. It arrived late that evening, where it remained until July 30, when ordered back to Harpers Ferry. On July 31, a portion of the regiment was ordered across the river into the defenses on Maryland Heights, the scene of their baptism by fire earlier that month. Several other companies were ordered to Frederick and Monocacy before arriving back at Harpers Ferry on August 7. The continuous marching and countermarching had debilitated much of the regiment. Many men were unable to stand the march from Halltown to Harpers Ferry and were left to straggle in small groups. John W. Osburn recalled after the war that "The weather was very hot through July...which made it very hard on the men marching, and a great many were sunstruck."[26] The record of events for

---

[24] *Belmont Chronicle*, September 29, 1864.
[25] Thomas C. Dungan to Elizabeth Dungan, July 31, 1862, Ken Mitchell private collection.
[26] *National Tribune*, February 25, 1892.

Company H details a forced march from Wolfsville, Maryland, through Frederick and on to Monocacy, a distance a twenty-two miles "without halting for food."[27] Benjamin Bogardus testified to the regiment's tribulations: "I know the marching was hard, as I went the last half of it without shoes."[28]

Unfortunately, the 170th's marching was not yet done. With Early's Confederates once again moving down the Shenandoah Valley on August 3, the 170th was ordered from Maryland Heights and into the rifle pits on Camp Hill above Harpers Ferry. One member of Company A described the place as "very dirty...& no wood to cook with." With Early's troops making no threatening movement against Harpers Ferry, more than 200 men of the 170th were detached to a convalescent camp in Knoxville, Maryland, on August 5. The war had taken its toll on these men, who only three months earlier had been in the safe confines of home.

While the 170th recuperated during that first week of August from a month of intense campaigning, the Union high command determined to put a halt to Early's operations in the Shenandoah Valley by establishing the Middle Military Division (popularly known as the Army of the Shenandoah). Now the largest Union army ever assembled in the Shenandoah Valley, approximately 40,000 men, was placed under command of Major General Philip H. Sheridan and poised to strike. As part of Sheridan's army the 170th Ohio would get little rest. On August 9, Sheridan ordered a general advance against Early. The 170th covered twenty miles on August 10, and camped at Berryville that evening. That day's march proved so demanding that some of the men had to be carted in ambulances. The next day's march was equally as difficult as the army marched cross-country to Millwood, the 170th drawing the assignment of guarding the division's wagon train. The regiment missed Colonel John Singleton Mosby's attack on Sheridan's wagon train at Berryville by a matter of hours, instead continuing on August 12, and reaching Cedar Creek where it remained through the following day.

By the third week of August the 170th had fulfilled ninety days of its term of service. National Guard regiments in Baltimore

---

[27] Janet Hewett, et. al., eds. *Supplement to the Official Records of the Union and Confederate Armies* (Wilmington, NC: Broadfoot Publishing, 1994-1998), pt. 2, vol. 56, 271.
[28] *National Tribune*, February 25, 1892.

and Washington, D.C., were transferred back to Ohio almost daily. The 170th started that process on August 14, when they were ordered back to Harpers Ferry. Covering eighteen miles on August 14, they camped for the night at Winchester, continuing twenty-three miles to Harpers Ferry the following day where the regiment encamped at Bolivar Heights. The march back to Harpers Ferry was made without rations being issued, Sheridan's command being short on rations following Mosby's attack on the wagon train at Berryville. John Osburn related that the men had to "live on green corn with a little poor fresh beef."[29] Soaring temperatures further added to the misery. One soldier recalled that "the scorching sun of August made the beautiful groves in the Valley 'way marks' to which we look forward with ardent joy, hoping that one of the fine springs...was close at hand."[30]

It was during this march that Lewis Lewton, Captain of Company K, was promoted to colonel of the 170th. Lieutenant Colonel Arthur Higgins had done an admirable job leading the regiment through engagements at Maryland Heights, Cool Spring, and Second Kernstown. Lewton would shepherd his command back to Ohio to be mustered out of service.

"The 170th is home"

On August 17, 1864, Special Order No. 150 stated that all Ohio National Guard troops serving within the Department of West Virginia be sent home.[31] The 170th spent the next week in camp at Bolivar Heights awaiting transportation. When an ambulance full of wounded soldiers was captured at Halltown on August 19, the 170th was dispatched to the area for guard duty, capturing three prisoners in the process. The regiment moved to Bolivar the following day, remaining there under arms as Early tested Sheridan's strength at Charles Town and Summit Point. On the evening of August 24, transportation was secured and the regiment boarded train cars for Baltimore. At long last the 170th was headed home.

From Baltimore the regiment took a train to Pittsburgh. It

---

[29] *National Tribune*, January 21, 1892.
[30] *Belmont Chronicle*. September 29, 1864.
[31] O.R. ser. 1, vol. 43, pt. 1, 826.

arrived there the following evening and received a meal at Soldiers Rest. One soldier recalled "our trip home was a pleasant one to all," and that the accommodations and provisions at Pittsburgh were "the best the city affords," excelling Washington, Baltimore, and Columbus.[32] Two men from the regiment died of disease during the stop in Pittsburgh. The regiment continued to Ohio the next day. When the 170th Ohio arrived in Columbus on August 28, they were assigned to Camp Chase.

Grave of William C. McNary, Belmont, Ohio
McNary died in Pittsburgh on September 2, 1864
(*Photo by Tom Buckley*)

The regiment encamped at Camp Chase for the next two weeks. During this time, they turned over their muskets and equipment and received their final pay. On September 10, the regiment was officially mustered out of Union service and began the trip home to eastern Ohio. Several veterans of the 170th chose to reenlist for further service in the 193rd Ohio. Service in the 193rd took them back to Harpers Ferry and Winchester performing guard and garrison duty in the spring of 1865.

Several weeks after the regiment's service officially ended, one of its veterans succinctly summed up all the unit endured

---

[32] *Belmont Chronicle*, September 29, 1864

during its 100 days:

> *The 170th is home. We have seen some hard service. All of us will know what it is to be a soldier; what the denials and sufferings of the soldiers are; what we owe our brethren who have and are enduring 'the burden and heat of the day'; and we can all read the 'war news' more intelligently than we have ever done. None of us will regret our experience, or be willing to part with what we have learned in the short time we have been in the field.*[33]

---

[33] *Belmont Chronicle*, September 29, 1864.

"Uncle John Bowman's and His Uncle Sam and Their Families are Going to Ohio"
Sheridan's Refugee Wagon Train

Prue Engle Yelinek

On Sunday, September 25, 1864, Major General Philip H. Sheridan's Army of the Shenandoah marched into Harrisonburg, Virginia. Three days earlier Sheridan's command soundly defeated Confederate general Jubal A. Early's Army of the Valley at Fisher's Hill. While Early's battered command retreated south to Brown's Gap in the Blue Ridge Mountains, Sheridan established headquarters at the home of Captain Abraham Byrd and contemplated his next move. Over the next several days, Sheridan resisted Lieutenant General Ulysses S. Grant's requests that the Army of the Shenandoah move further south and open the way to Charlottesville and Lynchburg. Instead, Sheridan convinced Grant that it was more strategically beneficial to make a retrograde movement, north, down the Valley, carrying out Grant's insistence that Sheridan make a wasteland of the fertile Shenandoah Valley, destroying or appropriating everything that could be used to sustain the Confederate war effort. What resulted was nearly two weeks of plunder and devastation in various parts of Rockingham, Shenandoah, Augusta, and Page counties that came to be known as the Burning.[1]

Approximately one month later, Bettie Neff Miller wrote her sister Sue describing what happened around her home near Bridgewater, seven miles south of Harrisonburg.[2]

---

[1] For a complete study of the Burning see John L. Heatwole, *The Burning; Sheridan's Devastation of the Shenandoah Valley* (Charlottesville, VA: Rockbridge Publishing, 1998).

[2] Bettie Neff Miller to Sue (Susan) Neff, October 29, 1864, typescript copy in possession of the author. Bettie and Sue were daughters of Elder John and Catherine Wine Neff of Rude's Hill, Shenandoah County, VA.

> *I suppose you have already been apprised of their burning here in Rockingham but I'll mention some of the buildings, John Herons house and barn John R Moore's house & barn Coffman's barn   Moomaw's house and barn   Christian Garbers house and barn Mr. Swope's house & barn David Gerber Gerber's house and barn. Blosser's Winger's [sic] John Flory's Hashbargers (sic) and Widow Miller's house and barn and so many others I could'nt mention them[.]*

In addition to the houses and barns of friends and neighbors, Bettie added that "Cousin Dan Bowman's mill" was burned and that their "Uncle John Bowman's and his Uncle Sam and their families have gone to Ohio... and a great many other families"[3]

Uncle John Bowman and these "many other families," to whom Bettie referred, were part of what has come to be known as Sheridan's refugee wagon train, an exodus of Valley residents that took place the first week of October 1864, in the midst of the Burning. In uncharacteristic concern for the Valley's victims of this "hard war" Sheridan offered to provide an empty army supply wagon and team to anyone who wished to leave the devastated area. Those who desired to go were promised guarded passage to safety to the North.[4]

While Sheridan's offer was open to anyone, it proved to be an opportunity most utilized by the large population of Dunkers and Mennonites concentrated in Rockingham and adjoining counties whose prosperous farms spread across the area.[5] Although

---

[3] David S. Rodes and Norman R. Wenger, eds., *Unionists and the Civil War Experience in the Shenandoah Valley* (Dayton, VA: Valley Research Associates, 2009), 5: 578, 560, 598, 618; David S. Rodes and Norman R. Wenger, eds., *Unionists and the Civil War Experience in the Shenandoah Valley* (Dayton, VA: Valley Research Associates, 2005), 3: 334, 348. John Bowman and his second wife, Rebecca Wine Bowman (sister of Bettie and Sue Neff's mother, Catherine), lived on a large farm one and one-half miles south of Harrisonburg on the west side of Warm Springs Turnpike. By 1864, the farm had been divided among three of their sons: Isaac, John Wine, and Joseph. Two other sons who lived near Dayton, Benjamin and Daniel, owned what is today the Silver Lake Mill, which was burned. Their youngest son, Samuel, had been sent north. All were German Baptist Brethren (Dunkers). John Bowman's "Uncle Sam" is not yet identified.

[4] Peter S. Hartman, *Reminiscences of the Civil War* (Lancaster, PA: Eastern Mennonite Libraries and Archives, 1964), 24; Rodes and Wenger, eds., *Unionists*, 3: 934. Also see Heatwole, *Burning*, 62.

[5] Dunker, Tunker, and Dunkard were terms commonly used to refer to German Baptist Brethren or Brethren (today's Church of the Brethren). The term referred to their practice

the events of late September and early October intensified the vulnerability of these two groups, their prevalence among the refugees can be traced to factors that existed long before Sheridan's arrival.

Prior to the Civil War, the religious beliefs of both Dunkers and Mennonites placed them in a minority among the country's populace. While some differences in doctrine and practice distinguished the two, both were considered "historic peace churches" whose members held in common Christian principles of strong opposition to both slavery and participation in war. In addition to these two foundational faith beliefs, both groups held an inherent sense of loyalty to the federal government and opposed dissolution of the Union. As the country's sectional crisis escalated, their fear and foreboding was reflected in the January 1, 1861, diary entry of Dunker leader, Elder John Kline:

> *The year opens with dark and lowering clouds in our national horizon. I feel a deep interest in the peace and prosperity of our country; but in my view, both are sorely threatened now. Secession is the cry farther south; and I greatly fear its poisonous breath is being wafted northward towards Virginia on the wings of finatical [sic] discontent. A move is clearly on hand for holding a convention at Richmond, Virginia; and while its advocates publicly deny the charge, I, for one, feel sure that it signals the separation of our beloved old State from the family in which she has long lived and been happy... Secession means war; and war means tears and ashes and blood. It means bonds and imprisonments, and perhaps even death to many in our beloved Brotherhood, who, I have the confidence to believe, will die, rather than disobey God by taking arms.*[6]

The future that Kline feared began to take shape with the Virginia Secession Convention's vote to sever bonds with the United States on April 17, 1861. By the time the statewide referendum

---

of trine immersion or "dunking" three times at baptism.
[6] Benjamin Funk, ed., *Life and Labors of Elder John Kline the Martyr Missionary* (Elgin, IL: Brethren Publishing House, 1900), 438.

on secession occurred on May 23, those suspected of being loyal to the Union were being threatened by their aggressive and disapproving secessionist neighbors. Threats of bodily harm, even murder, confiscation or destruction of property, and being driven out of the county were loudly voiced. As Dunker Bishop Solomon Garber, a leader in the Cook's Creek congregation, remembered: "all Union men were in fear from the threats of violence made generally against any who opposed secession or who should refuse to vote for it. I was threatened with arrest and was reported to the Provost Marshall... Union men did not feel safe to vote their sentiments and very few did."[7]

For Dunkers and Mennonites who had been able to escape antebellum compulsory militia service by paying a small fine, the full impact of what war would mean for them came when Virginia enacted a military conscription law in July 1861. Peter Hartman described the shock and despair that swept through his Mennonite community when "on a Sunday at Weavers Church while there was preaching a captain came and there notified every man between the ages of eighteen and forty-five to report for war." As the officer turned and strode out of the church, the entire congregation dissolved in tears.[8]

Faced with conscription, Dunker, and to a lesser extent Mennonite, leaders immediately began a long and difficult process to gain exemptions for their members. Changing laws and conflicting decisions by Virginia and the Confederate government complicated these efforts. Finally, on October 11, 1862, the Confederate Congress passed a law providing exemption from military service for members of "the society of Friends, and the Association of Dunkards, Nazarenes, and Mennonites."[9] But after a year and a half of war, even the hard-won exemptions did not eliminate the difficulties and dangers these faith communities

---

[7] Rodes and Wenger, eds., *Unionists*, 5: 138.
[8] Hartman, *Reminiscences*, 8.
[9] For a thorough discussion of Brethren and Mennonite involvement in securing exemptions see Roger E. Sappington, *The Brethren in Virginia: The History of the Church of the Brethren in Virginia* (Harrisonburg, VA: The Committee for Brethren History in Virginia, 1973), 69-76; D. H. Zigler, *History of the Brethren in Virginia* (Elgin IL: Brethren Publishing House, 1914), 94-126; James O. Leaman and Steven M. Nolt, *Mennonite, Amish, and the American Civil War* (Baltimore: The Johns Hopkins University Press, 2007), 60-66.

faced.

The new law required that each exempted man either furnish a substitute or pay $500 plus two percent of his taxable property to the government, nearly impossible for many. Hiring substitutes was expensive and often went against individual conscience and church polity. Paying the $500 fee plus tax challenged both personal and denominational monetary resources. Most Dunkers and Mennonites did not join their respective churches until their late teens or early twenties, or even after marriage, so most of their young men were not baptized members when the law was passed and thus not exempt. This forced them to face an array of difficult choices. Some who could afford it, and believed it their only option, hired substitutes. Others joined the Confederate army, often against parental and church approval. Examples exist of Dunkers or Mennonites who joined the military and later deserted, or were assigned as teamsters and cooks because of their refusal to shoot when in combat. Many who refused to comply with conscription were physically carried off from homes or fields and taken to Confederate camps. Others risked capture and imprisonment by attempting to escape to northern soil. Two groups of Dunkers and Mennonites were captured and imprisoned in early 1862 before Virginia's first exemption law was passed. Many literally chose to go into hiding in local homes and barns or created area mountain hideouts.

Dunkers and Mennonites continued to struggle with these choices through the remainder of 1862 and 1863. Then, on February 17, 1864, the Confederate Congress passed a new law designed to bolster the ranks of the Confederate army. This law continued previous exemptions, but extended eligibility to "all able-bodied men between the ages of 17 and 50."[10] This put at risk even greater numbers of young non-members as well as older ones now unable to pay the required "tax" because of war's deprivations. Often older men were the only ones left to manage farms and provide for their families because sons, other relatives, and even hired hands were hiding or fled north.

---

[10] Sappington, *The Brethren*, 80.

These internal pressures were matched by constant external pressures as supporters of the Confederacy lost patience with their pro-Union, non-combatant neighbors who continued to seek military service exemptions or escape north. Such antagonism reached a zenith with the assassination of Elder John Kline. Well-known and already widely criticized for his opposition to slavery, war, and secession, Kline, who lived in Broadway, Virginia, regularly crossed enemy lines to attend national church meetings as far west as Indiana and engage in preaching missions in Maryland, Pennsylvania, West Virginia, and Ohio. Such movement aroused suspicions that he was a spy. Soon after returning from attending the Brethren Annual Meeting in Indiana, he was ambushed and murdered by area partisans on June 15, 1864. Harrisonburg's *Rockingham Register* weakly characterized the killing as "lawless" and a "tragedy," but strongly criticized Kline's "erroneous views" and "antagonism...to the Confederacy."[11]

With Sheridan's arrival on September 25, Dunkers, Mennonites, other area Unionists, and non-Confederate sympathizers were thrust into even greater vulnerability. Troops from Major General Horatio Wright's Sixth Corps, Major General George Crook's Army of West Virginia (Eighth Corps) and Major General William Emory's Nineteenth Corps spread out in camps around Harrisonburg that extended south of the town along the Valley Pike and southwest along the Warm Springs Turnpike toward Dayton. That evening, portions of Major General Alfred Torbert's three late-arriving cavalry divisions over-ran the farm of Mennonite David Hartman on a hill northwest of Harrisonburg. In their wake, the horsemen left "thirty fat hogs...the chickens and about thirty or forty sheep" shot dead."[12] Such slaughter was indicative of what was to follow.

During the next week-and-a-half, farms and homes of Union loyalists and Confederate sympathizers alike were plundered for food and forage. Livestock continued to be slaughtered in pastures and barnyards or rounded up and driven away to Union camps. Miles of rail fences fueled thousands of army camp fires. Valuable

---

[11] Leaman and Nolt, *Mennonites*, 189-190; Sappington, *The Brethren,* 81-84.
[12] Hartman, *Reminiscences*, 24.

and indispensable horses were stolen from stables and fields. A young Mennonite pastor, David H. Landis, later explained: "We were, for the last four years, living in a somewhat disturbed and uneasy state of mind... in consequence of the national calamity that is now existing. In the later part of September, the "calamity grew severe." He pictured the Union army "sweeping everything before them like a wild hurricane: there was nothing left to eat for man or beast; neither was there anything for beasts, as they left no beast from horse down to the chickens: all was taken."[13] But the real horror was still to come.

On September 26, portions of Brigadier General Wesley Merritt's cavalry rode south and east from the Harrisonburg area to Port Republic, Staunton, and Waynesboro, with orders to destroy government supplies and damage the Central Virginia Railroad. These raids were only partially successful because of confrontations with Confederate troops in the area. However, the Union horsemen were also ordered to burn barns filled with grain and to slaughter or collect livestock as they returned to their camps. Destruction once widely spread out and "generally sporadic" in the Valley during late summer and early fall now "became daily" as "the torch-bearing Yankees poured into the heart of the region."[14]

Michael Shank, another Mennonite pastor and farmer who lived five miles south of Harrisonburg on the Valley Pike, described this transition in what he called "our troubles:"

> *When General Sheridan's army came into the Valley of Va., about the last of September, the 'Boys' or prowlers, contrary to the Generals orders, commenced pilfering, robbing, and plundering; squads of them would go to citizens houses in almost frantic appearances, their very faces speaking terror to the inhabitants, while they were searching every room form cellar to garret, breaking open bureau drawers, chests and closets, taking whatever suited their fancy, such as Money, watches, jewelry,*

---

[13] D.H. Landis to Daniel Brenneman, October 30,1864, published in *Herald of Truth*, December 1864.
[14] Jeffry D. Wert, *From Winchester to Cedar Creek: The Shenandoah Campaign of 1864* (Carlisle, PA: South Mountain Press, 1987), 158.

wearing apparel &c, at the same time threatening to shoot the inmates of the house if they followed after them.[15]

While this was going on inside the house, outside in barnyards, out-buildings, and pastures, soldiers seized Shank's livestock, including horses, cows, and cattle. As the troops continued their march toward Staunton, thousands of feet and hooves tramped through Shank's corn and grain fields. "Thus they continued their work of destruction until they reached Staunton or its vicinity, from whence they commenced retreating, and burning barns, mills, &c. For several days before we left we saw great columns of smoke rising like dark clouds almost from one mountain to the other."[16]

Union cavalry raids continued during the last days of September as they again burned barns and mills and killed or drove off livestock in northern Augusta and southern Rockingham counties. On Thursday, September 29, cartographer Jedediah Hotchkiss, riding with General Early whose troops were south of the Union position and painfully aware of the destruction, noted that the enemy made "the night light with burning barns, haystacks, &c." The next day he added that the "Yankees went to Bridgewater yesterday."[17]

Bettie Neff Miller was doing laundry around noon when many of those Yankee troops overran the Miller farm. She quit her washing and "waited upon their persons until I hadn't any for myself." In addition to the food she provided, the soldiers took all her bread, pies, milk, cream, seven turkeys, and all the cows "but two of them came back." Bettie also complained that they took the only good tin cup she had. As the marauding troops moved on they broke yard, meadow, and field fences on the Miller property. For Bettie, the presence of these enemy troops made her world "the most intolerable place mortal man or woman ever lived in." But, she realized, "we escaped well considering their behavior towards the

---

[15] Michael Shank to Brother Funk, November 19, 1864, published in *Herald of Truth*, December 1864

[16] Ibid.; Rodes and Wenger, eds., *Unionists,* 3: 543-544.

[17] Archie P. McDonald, ed., *Make Me a Map of The Valley: The Civil War Journal of Stonewall Jackson's Topographer* (Dallas: Southern Methodist University Press, 1973), 234.

citizens the other side of Bridgewater."[18]

North of Bridgewater, residents could see the rising columns of smoke south and east of them, while their fields and barns continued to be stripped of the year's harvest and cellars and smokehouses emptied of foods prepared for the coming winter. It was sometime during these days of late September that Sheridan made the decision to offer free wagon transportation and safe passage for area citizens caught in the midst of his destructive campaign.

There was immediate and wide-spread response to his offer. On October 2, artist James Taylor sketched a sizeable group of men gathered at General Crook's headquarters near Harrisonburg. Commissary W. H. Douglas is shown in the midst of the group "giving the refugees information how to reach friends and where to fall in with the supply train that was to proceed down the Valley when night closed." Taylor estimated there were about one hundred Dunkers and Mennonites, who he described as "peace-loving" and "non-combatant," gathered there to receive passes for the wagon train. Aware of the tensions that existed between "Southern sympathizing neighbors and these non-combatant Unionists," Taylor's comments on his sketch acknowledged the fear of "what was in store for them at the hands of the Confederates if the Federals were compelled to fall back."[19]

D. H. Landis, whose house and farm had been vandalized and plundered, applied for his pass at the provost marshal's office on South Court Square in Harrisonburg. There he met Benjamin Wenger, his son Abraham, and "several other of the Brethren (Mennonites)...making preparations to leave."[20] It was ironic that their passes were issued from the place where, until recently, Confederate military scouts were dispatched to search for and arrest Rebel army deserters, as well as non-combatants who were trying to escape conscription.

Among the latter were Peter Hartman and six of his close friends who were now eligible for military service. Deciding this

---

[18] Bettie Neff Miller to Sue (Susan) Neff, October 29, 1864, typescript copy in possession of the author.
[19] Hartman, *Reminiscences,* 13; Rodes and Wenger, eds., *Unionists,* 3: x; Leaman and Nolt, *Mennonites,* 209.
[20] D.H. Landis to Daniel Brenneman, October 30, 1864, published in *Herald of Truth,* December 1864.

was the time to go north, they turned themselves over to Union soldiers and were taken to army headquarters. There they were interviewed by Sheridan who Hartman described as "the most savage-looking man I think I ever saw." Despite his looks, Sheridan approved their requests and even added separate passes for their horses.[21]

In the midst of all this movement and turmoil, an already difficult situation changed dramatically. Early in the morning of October 3, Sheridan's twenty-two-year-old chief engineer, Lieutenant John Rogers Meigs, son of Quartermaster General Montgomery M. Meigs, and two assistants set out from headquarters in a light drizzle to conduct a survey of the area. By afternoon, Meigs and his companions had secured the help of two Dunker minister-farmers, John Flory and Joseph Harshbarger, brothers-in-law, whose adjoining farms were approximately four miles south of Harrisonburg, between the Warm Springs Turnpike and Valley Pike. Both Unionists, Flory had taken Meigs "to the top of a high hill" where "they had viewed the country with field glass and spent an hour or more together." Harshbarger spent his time with Meigs pointing out various mountain passes near his farm, which the engineer "sketched down and mapped." Perhaps in return for his help, Meigs agreed to give Harshbarger a voucher for two horses that had been taken from his farm a few days before. The young officer told the Dunker to meet him that evening and he would bring the voucher. Harshbarger followed through and waited at the designated time and place.[22] Meigs never came.

Earlier that afternoon, three Confederate scouts sent to determine Union troop placements, moved into the area where Lt. Meigs was surveying. One of them, Franklin "Frank" Shaver, had been reared in the area and as dusk fell, Shaver and his companions were trying to reach his family home. They were riding on the Swift Gap Road about a mile north of Dayton when Lt. Meigs and his men, returning from their surveying, turned right off the Warm Springs Turnpike onto the same road and found themselves riding about thirty yards behind the scouts. By then the early morning drizzle had turned into a steady rain and the Confederates were

---

[21] Hartman, *Reminiscences*, 24-25.
[22] For the Flory-Harshbarger encounters with Meigs see Rodes and Wenger, eds., *Unionists*, 5: 141,144-145.

wearing water-proof ponchos that concealed their uniforms. Meigs and his men gradually caught up with the trio and ordered them to stop. Accounts vary as to what happened when the two groups met, but there was gunfire and Meigs lay dead on the road. In the confusion, one of the assistant surveyors was wounded and captured. The scouts and their captive fled back to Confederate lines, while the other assistant escaped and made his way back to Sheridan's headquarters where he reported that the lieutenant had been killed by local bushwhackers.[23]

Hearing this, Sheridan flew into a rage. Guerilla bands and bushwhackers had been the bane of his campaign since coming to the Valley in August. His supply trains were constantly attacked and his soldiers ambushed and ruthlessly killed by partisan rangers. Now Sheridan was told that some of them had killed this promising young officer who had become very special to him.

Believing that Meigs had been murdered by guerillas who were probably harbored by local citizens, the angry and grieving Sheridan called for swift and severe revenge. He ordered "all houses within an area of five miles (of the killing site) to be burned."[24] As well as farms, this radius included the small town of Dayton. Brigadier General George Custer, who had been promoted to command of the third cavalry division just days before and whose headquarters was at Dayton, was tasked with carrying out the directive.

Within hours of the young engineer's death, flames erupted as the men of Custer's Fifth New York Cavalry set to work. "One of the first places targeted was the farm of Noah and Sarah Wenger, just fifty yards from the spot where Meigs had been killed. Having endured days of continuing predation on their farm, the Wengers had already left. That night their barn was destroyed, but their house was later saved by a hired hand.[25] About a mile away on the west side of the Warm Springs Turnpike, young Peter Blosser was present "the evening when they burnt the buildings" on the family farm. "The barn was burnt first, all the outbuildings, and the house

---

[23] For accounts of Meigs' death see Heatwole, *Burning*, 89-92; Wert, *From Winchester to Cedar Creek*, 145; Leaman and Nolt, *Mennonites*, 204.
[24] Philip H. Sheridan, *Personal Memoirs of P.H. Sheridan* (New York: Charles L. Webster & Co., 1888) 2: 52.
[25] Rodes and Wenger, eds., *Unionists*, 3: 578.

with "fire in every room."[26]

As all of this occurred, Michael Shank and his family were making their way to Harrisonburg in the pouring rain. He had watched the flames from previous days' burning south of their home come closer and closer. When fires were within one-and-a-half mile, he and his family chose to leave rather than endure "the terrors already inflicted upon us, as well as the fate which was yet awaiting us." On the afternoon of October 3, he had gone to one of the designated camps and applied for two teams, which arrived at his home around 3:00 p.m. Packing "bed clothes, wearing apparel, some dishes, and a few other articles," but "leaving nearly all our house furnishings," the family left well after dark and traveled five miles north to Harrisonburg where they spent the night.[27]

In the early morning hours of October 4, with smoke and fire in the air, citizens of Dayton were awakened and informed that their town was to be burned that evening. After an anxious day, Lieutenant Colonel Thomas F. Wildes, 116th Ohio Infantry, refused to carry out the order. A veteran of the 116th Ohio described Dayton as "the most loyal or at least the most innocent of any place I have seen in the Valley."[28] Although Wildes' effort saved Dayton, an estimated thirty houses in the immediate area were destroyed.

While the town of Dayton was spared, burning of homes, barns, and mills continued throughout the day in the designated five-mile radius. Michael Shank, who was waiting with his family in Harrisonburg, decided to go back to his farm where he "found the destruction complete: the dwelling house and barn, with all their contents and all their outbuildings were entirely consumed by the flames."[29] Others continued to lose their homes and farms through the next two days. "The Burnt District" as it became known, reached north from the site of Meigs' death to Harrisonburg, east to just beyond the Valley Pike, south to Bridgewater, west to the Dry River area and north again, passing on the east side of the local landmark,

---

[26] Trenton Greenwalt, "A History of the Jonas Blosser House and Barn" unpublished honors project, Bridgewater College, January 4, 2002. This is reprinted in Rodes and Wenger, eds., *Unionists*, 3: 599.

[27] Michael Shank to Brother Funk, November 19, 1864, published in *Herald of Truth*, December 1864.

[28] William T. Patterson Diary, October 4, 1864, Ohio Historical Society, Columbus, OH, quoted in Leaman and Nolt, *Mennonite*, 205.

[29] Michael Shank to Brother Funk, November 19, 1864, published in *Herald of Truth*, December 1864.

"Mole Hill," to the Rawley Springs Turnpike, which ran east into Harrisonburg.[30]

Even before this latest eruption of devastation and chaos, area citizens were leaving. After securing his pass and a horse, Peter Hartman went home to get a saddle, after which he returned to Harrisonburg where he and his friends spent Sunday night, October 2, sleeping under wagons in an area designated for refugees. The next morning, they started "to go north."[31] David Landis, who earlier had met fellow Mennonites, Benjamin and Abraham Wenger at the provost office, also left his home on October 2, and went to Harrisonburg with a "U.S. Government supplied" six-mule-team wagon packed with family clothing and bedding. He and his family left Harrisonburg "at 8 o'clock on the 3rd."[32] The Landis family, numerous members of the Wenger family, Peter Hartman, and his companions were apparently part of the first organized group of refugees to leave with wagons supplied by Sheridan. The day and time of departure corresponds to the comments of artist James Taylor that the supply train "was to proceed down the Valley when night closed."[33] After leaving Harrisonburg, Landis chronicled their journey:

> [We] traveled slowly down the pike, stopping often and sometimes for a considerable while; but we knew not for what purpose. We arrived a few miles below New Market after dark and it rained very hard, so that our bed clothes got considerable wet. We left here on the 4th and arrived at Woodstock at dusk. On this day we had some trouble, as the guerillas of the South had burnt a bridge. On the 5th we left Woodstock and arrived at Newtown at 5 o'clock. Eight miles from Winchester, another bridge had been burnt on that day, by the rebels. On the 6th, we left Newtown and arrived at Winchester at 10 o'clock, where we laid over until the next day in the afternoon. On the 8th we arrived at Martinsburg.[34]

---

[30] Rodes and Wenger, eds., *Unionists*, 3:13.
[31] Hartman, *Reminiscence*, 25; Rodes and Wenger, eds., *Unionists*, 3: 934-935.
[32] D.H. Landis to Daniel Brenneman, October 30, 1864, published in *Herald of Truth*, December 1864.
[33] Leaman and Nolt in *Mennonites* give the date of the Taylor sketch as October 2, 1864.
[34] D.H. Landis to Daniel Brenneman, October 30, 1864, published in *Herald of Truth*,

A second group left two days later in the smoke-filled aftermath of the Meigs killing. On the first page of the red daybook Mennonite farmer and potter Emanuel Suter used as a diary, he wrote:

> *The federal army being in the Valley of Virginia, burning dwelling houses Mills, etc. as general destruction was threatened Myself and family decided to leave the Shenandoah Valley and go north. In the morning of the 5th day of October we left went to Harrisonburg then went with the army to Mt. Jackson, there we remained that night and all the way of the 6th.*[35]

Michael Shank and his family who had traveled to Harrisonburg in pouring rain on the night of October 3, and whose entire farm had been burned the next day, were among those who left with the Suters on Wednesday morning.[36]

Another group of refugees departed on the morning of Thursday, October 6, as Sheridan withdrew his army from the Harrisonburg area. Taking personal interest in the welfare of a prominent local Unionist sympathizer, "Sheridan sent an escort into Harrisonburg to meet Unionist Robert Gray and his family and shepherd them to the safety of the departure area. There they joined...hundreds of other civilians in a refugee train."[37]

With at least three separate departures recorded, Sheridan's "refugee wagon train" apparently was not a single aggregate group. Rather, there was a succession of refugees traveling in army supply wagons provided by Sheridan, moving under military guard from the Harrisonburg area to Martinsburg, West Virginia, over several days during the first week of October 1864.[38]

December 1864.
[35] Emanuel Suter Diary, 1, Menno Simons Historical Library and Archives, Eastern Mennonite University, Harrisonburg, VA.
[36] Michael Shank to Brother Funk, November 19, 1864, published in *Herald of Truth*, December 1864.
[37] Lewis L. Fisher, *No Cause of Offense: A Virginia Family of Union Loyalists Confronts the Civil War* (San Antonio, TX: Maverick Publishing Company, 2012): 53-54.
[38] Using the October 5 date for departure are Dale MacAllister, "The Great Refugee Wagon Train," *The Heritage Museum Newsletter* 37, no. 1 (2015): 4; and Rebecca Suter Lindsay, "Emanuel Suter Family: Refugees Sent North," *Shenandoah Mennonite Historian* 22, no. 4

Regardless of when they left, there is no official record of the number of refugees or wagons involved in this exodus. Sheridan later reported to Grant: "From the vicinity of Harrisonburg over 400 wagon loads of refugees have been sent back to Martinsburg; most of these people were Dunkers, and had been conscripted."[39] Peter Hartman described the white canvas-topped caravan with which he traveled as "a long train-1,600 wagons in our train-sixteen miles long."[40] Rebecca and George Lutz remembered traveling with what was said to be "1200 families... and ten hundred wagons in the train besides the wagons and carriages of the refugees."[41]

In addition to those who began their journey near Harrisonburg, many others who were walking, on horseback, or driving personal farm wagons and carriages joined the refugee trains as they moved northward. There were others who desired to leave and were prepared but were prevented at the last minute. Several families gathered at one location, packed and ready, "waiting together for the wagons to come, but there was none to show them the way." Samuel Hartman, a close neighbor of the John Bowman family, had made arrangements to go north with Sheridan's army, but, with his horses taken earlier by Union troops, was "unable to get a team" and consequently was "left behind."[42] One Union soldier remembered "hundreds of refugees accompanied us from Staunton, Mt. Crawford, and Harrisonburg. Unionists who had endured persecution until it was no longer endurable, and who now left houses and farms to find relief in the north from their sufferings and loyalty."[43]

Ahead of those who left on Wednesday, October 5, a single wagon under military escort carried Lieutenant Meigs' body down the Valley Pike to Martinsburg accompanied by Captain Thayer

---

(2014): 6. In the same issue Elwood L. Yoder, "Sheridan's 1864 Wagon Train, on page 2 indicates that families who desired safe passage "should come to Harrisonburg by October 6," but gives no source. Heatwole suggests refugee wagons left on both October 5 and 6. See Heatwole, *Burning*, 130, 184.

[39] O.R. ser. I, vol. 43, pt. 2, 308.
[40] Hartman, *Reminiscences*, 25-26.
[41] Rodes and Wenger, eds., *Unionists*, 1: 323. An article on Harper's Ferry states: "An average supply train included 1,000 wagons hitched to 6,000 mules and would stretch for more than ten miles." Dennis E. Frye, "Harper's Ferry: The Base of Operations for Sheridan's Valley Campaign," *The Sentinel* (2014): 44.
[42] Rodes and Wenger, eds., *Unionists*, 3: 602, 808; Rodes and Wenger, eds., *Unionists*, 5: 817.
[43] George T. Stevens, *Three Years in the Sixth Corps*, (Albany, NY: S.R. Gray Publisher, 1866), 411; Heatwole, *Burning*, 184.

Melvin of Sheridan's staff. From Martinsburg, Meigs' corpse was sent by train to Harpers Ferry and then to his home in Washington, D.C., where his funeral was held October 8.[44]

As the first group of refugees left Newtown and headed toward Winchester on Thursday morning, October 6, those who were with the second group awoke at their overnight camp in the vicinity of Mt. Jackson. Miles behind them, Union troops pulled out of their bivouacs around Harrisonburg and began their retrograde movement down the Valley. General Sheridan traveled with the infantry as they moved down the Valley Pike. About two hours later the cavalry followed. Custer's horsemen left their camps around Dayton and angled west, then north to the Back Road, which ran along the base of North Mountain. Two of Merritt's brigades traveled east of Custer, along the Broadway and Middle Roads that paralleled the Valley Pike, while a third brigade moved to their east along the Pike, spreading nearly to the base of the Massanutten. Additional cavalry under Colonel William Powell was on the eastern side of the Massanutten in Page County where it had been burning and raiding for several days. Thus, moving behind the rest of the army and the refugees, Sheridan's cavalry "spread across the Valley from the Blue Ridge to the eastern slope of the Allegheny's" and continued to burn crops, slaughter livestock, and confiscate Valley resources.[45] As the Union horsemen moved north, Confederate cavalry under Brigadier General Thomas L. Rosser pursued, enraged by the destruction. Late in the evening, Rosser's men caught up with Custer's rearguard near Brock's Gap where a "spirited skirmish ensued." The action kept Rosser at bay until night when Custer withdrew under cover of darkness.[46]

The refugees camped near Mt. Jackson remained stationary through October 6. Whether they were aware of all that was happening to the south and west is unknown. Having left so much behind, other immediate concerns were recorded in diaries and held in memory. Emanuel Suter took advantage of the delay to have his horses shod, noting that "they were barefooted and very tender."

---

[44] *O.R.*, ser. I, vol. 43, pt. 2, 74, 305, 314; Robert O'Harrow, Jr., *The Quartermaster Montgomery C. Meigs,* (New York: Simon & Schuster, 2016), 216.
[45] Sanford C. Kellogg, *The Shenandoah Valley and Virginia, 1861-1865* (New York: The Neale Publishing Company, 1903), 211.
[46] William N. McDonald, *A History of the Laurel Brigade: Originally the Ashby Cavalry of the Army of Northern Virginia* (Baltimore: The Johns Hopkins University Press, 2002), 301.

Later, as his family settled down for their second night, he took time to record those traveling with him: "wife, Elizabeth, three children, Daniel Reuben, Susan Virginia, and John Robert. Two little girls had died viz. Mary Margaret and Sarah Jane. The Sister Margaret Suter and Father Daniel Suter are with us." He noted his brother Christian and a young man named Albert Jenkins were "back in the rear but came to us on the way." The day's pause also allowed the Suters to connect with other families they knew from the Valley.[47] Over the course of the trip, Dunker and Mennonite families gathered together taking some comfort in familiar faces and available faith practices. Peter Hartman remembered that as weather permitted "quite a number of our own people...would get together in the evening and sing," This attracted the attention of soldiers who asked "if we were going to sing that night."[48]

As darkness fell on October 6, the Union infantry and third group of refugees reached the general area of the second refugee train encampment, and troop movements along the Valley Pike ceased. With infantry, artillery, supply and refugee wagons, ambulances, and herds of livestock being driven north with the army, the encampment stretched for approximately six miles, from near the Rockingham-Shenandoah County line below New Market, across Rude's Hill, and down into the wide, flat expanse of Meem's Bottom, nearly to the bridge at Mt. Jackson.[49]

Very early on the morning of October 7, Emanuel Suter recorded that orders were given to be ready to move out at "one o'clock." In the pre-dawn hours, a resident of Mt. Jackson, lying sick in bed, heard the sound of many wagons moving toward town. "Don't you hear the wagons," she asked a relative who was sitting with her. They alerted the household and gathered to watch as the refugee wagons "rumbled by in the darkness."[50] From Mt. Jackson, the pace of the wagon train quickened as refugees were pushed to

---

[47] Suter Diary, 1, 2.
[48] Hartman, *Reminiscences*, 26.
[49] Heatwole, *Burning*, 194, 195. Sheridan's headquarters that night was at the home of Elder John Neff, father of Bettie and Sue, located on a small rise beside a curve in the North Fork of the Shenandoah River, just below Rude's Hill. See Joseph Floyd Wine, *Life Along Holman's Creek* (Stephen's City, VA: Commercial Press, 1985), 53-54. In her letter, Bettie wrote "I heard that fathers barn was not burned." While there, Sheridan found partisan John McNeill, who had been mortally wounded on October 3, being cared for in a nearby home. McNeill was taken into Union custody and later died in Harrisonburg.
[50] Ibid., 201.

"a fast walk," but mostly Emanuel Suter found himself moving his team at a trot. He realized it was good he had yesterday's chance to shoe his horses.[51] Behind the refugees, the Union infantry moved out at dawn and headed toward Woodstock as the cavalry continued burning and rounding up livestock. Another attack by Rosser on Custer's forces near Mill Creek resulted in the Confederates taking some prisoners, recovering some of the livestock being driven by Custer's men, and capturing nine portable forges.

With distance growing between the groups of refugee wagons moving on the Valley Pike and cavalry skirmishes on the Back Road, it is difficult to correlate any of these engagements with references to fighting and gunfire recorded by refugees. In his memoir, Peter Hartman noted that as they traveled up the Pike, "one afternoon the guns began to cracking on the west of us not far away," with bullets passing through the canvas covers of the wagons. A man not identified as either soldier or refugee was brought to the train who had been "shot through the head." Peter was asked to help provide first aid.[52] Another refugee, Dunker Benjamin A. Sandy, traveling with Custer's wagons, was captured by Confederates near Mt. Jackson. His wagon and team were confiscated and Sandy was separated from his family. He was taken back to Harrisonburg by some of the Confederates, but later escaped with a group of Mennonites through the mountains to West Virginia and eventually was reunited with his family in Wheeling.[53]

Such incidents could also have been associated with the constant harassment by bushwhackers and partisans operating in the area about which Sheridan so bitterly complained. Reaching Cedar Creek for encampment on the evening of the 7th, Emanuel Suter recorded trouble keeping his horses from being stolen, forcing him and his father to spend the night guarding them. One would-be-thief "cut the halter strap while in Father's hand, but found that he was seen and got away quickly." Such harassment continued the rest of the way to Martinsburg.[54]

Peter Hartman echoed this problem: "We had to watch our

---

[51] Suter Diary, 2.
[52] Hartman, *Reminiscences*, 26.
[53] Rhodes and Wenger, eds., *Unionists*, 3:500.
[54] Suter Diary, 2-3.

horses," then added the additional concern of not only keeping horses but feeding them. His Christian conscience weighed in remembering a time when he and fellow refugee Sam Showalter stole hay from a barn along the way. "That worried me for a long time," Hartman confessed, but found solace as he remembered "when Christ went through the fields and plucked the ears of corn."[55]

While Hartman and the first group of refugees spent much of October 7 in Winchester, and the combined second and third group traveled to Cedar Creek, Sheridan and the infantry camped at Woodstock. From there he wired Grant notifying him of the destruction he had brought to the region and the "over 400 wagon loads of refugees" he had sent to Martinsburg. Looking ahead, he informed Grant, "I will continue the destruction of wheat, forage, etc. down to Fisher's Hill. When this is completed, the Valley from Winchester up to Staunton, 92 miles, will have but little in it for man or beast."[56]

Saturday morning, October 8, dawned cold and windy with occasional showers of rain and sleet throughout the day. The Suters left the encampment at Cedar Creek and moved "like the day before, mostly at a trot" passing through Winchester and on to Bunker Hill where they camped.[57] Further ahead some from the first group of refugees were already pulling their wagons into Martinsburg. Brigadier General John D. Stevenson, commanding the Military District at Harpers Ferry, wired Secretary of War Edwin Stanton: "General Sheridan's trains for supplies have arrived at Martinsburg with 169 rebel prisoners and large numbers of destitute refugees seeking homes in Pennsylvania and Ohio. Shall I finish transportation on Government's account? We ought to get rid of them." Stanton's quick reply was more sympathetic: "You are authorized to furnish transportation to destitute loyal citizens.[58]

As officials in Martinsburg began to deal with the first wave of refugees, Sheridan's infantry left Woodstock with orders to proceed to Strasburg. Custer continued along the Back Road. All of Merritt's brigades had now come together on the Valley Pike, still

---

[55] Hartman, *Reminiscences*, 25-26.
[56] O.R., ser. I, vol. 43, pt. 2, 308.
[57] Suter Diary, 3.
[58] OR, ser. I, vol. 43, pt. 2, 321.

involved with burning barns and crops and wrestling livestock. The day brought more sharp cavalry skirmishing as Rosser continued to harass Custer on the Back Road and Major General Lunsford L. Lomax, who had been trailing Merritt on the Pike, became more aggressive. Fuming and frustrated with these rear guard actions, on the night of the eighth, Sheridan ordered his cavalry commander to plan a counter attack on the Confederates the following morning, telling Torbert to "start out at daylight and whip the rebel cavalry or get whipped."[59]

That same night, as the Suters and many of their fellow refugees shivered in the cold at Bunker Hill, Peter Hartman and his companions pushed ahead on horseback. They joined the swelling number of refugees at Martinsburg, arriving "about midnight on Saturday."[60] The next morning, as Sheridan watched the cavalry battle at Tom's Brook from Round Top Mountain, the Suters set out again, traveling the last twelve miles from Bunker Hill to Martinsburg where they arrived at 3:00 p.m." There they and many of their fellow refugees spent another cold night out in the open.[61] Earlier in the day, Torbert's troops soundly defeated Rosser and Lomax and sent them reeling twenty-six miles back to Mt. Jackson in what became known as "The Woodstock Races." After halting the army to watch the battle, Sheridan ordered his troops to move into camp at Strasburg.

By the evening of October 9, the orchestrated destruction of the lower Shenandoah Valley ended while the rail yards and open areas around Martinsburg, West Virginia, teemed with soldiers, wagons, and growing numbers of refugees who now faced the task of making arrangements to travel to other places of safety in the north. The scene would have been much like that reported later by a *New York Post* correspondent: "The railroad, new built and surrounded with tons and tons of heated and twisted rails from former raids, was now lined with refugee families... The Government gives them transportation for themselves and their effects, and rations to keep them from starving." He estimated that through the month of October the Shenandoah Valley was "cleaned out" at the rate of "fifty or sixty families a day."[62]

---

[59] McDonald, *Laurel Brigade*, 305-306.
[60] Hartman, *Reminiscences*, 26.
[61] Suter Diary, 3.
[62] *Wheeling Daily Intelligencer*, November 3, 1864.

Peter Hartman watched the refugee wagons being unloaded and their contents transferred to waiting trains, later admitting that it was the first time this Shenandoah Valley farm boy had ever seen "a railroad engine and cars." He would not board one. Still in possession of a horse, he left Martinsburg and rode all the way to Hagerstown, Maryland.[63]

On Monday, October 10, the Suters moved from their first encampment to an area near an "Old Sawmill" where they met "a great many more families moving north and west," all apparently waiting to be processed and awarded a place on available trains.[64] They may have been in the area "of fifty acres or more" where the *Post* correspondent also reported seeing "hundreds of families of the Valley of Shenandoah," clustered around bright coal fires in the chilly nights. Around them were grouped the few household articles-chests, bureaus, and tables "which like the children of Israel they carried with them from out of Egypt."[65]

As part of the processing, each refugee was required to take an oath of allegiance to the United States government. All received a receipt certifying that they had done so. Margaret Suter apparently valued hers. After her death, the slip of paper which attested her having taken the oath was found among her personal papers. At the bottom was written: "refugee sent north."[66]

On October 12, the Suters moved into Maryland where the women and children took a train to Lancaster, Pennsylvania. The Suter men, along with the Albert Fishback family, continued "cross-country" with their horses, wagons, and carriages, and later joined the rest of the family.[67] Michael Shank and his family went to Lancaster, Pennsylvania, where they were living in late November "principally upon the charity of the brethren (Mennonites)."[68] David Landis and his family departed Martinsburg on the morning of October 10, and went by train to Wheeling. After making several more connections, they reached Bremen, Ohio by the end of

---

[63] Hartman, *Reminiscences*, 26.
[64] Suter Diary, 4.
[65] *Wheeling Daily Intelligencer*, November 3, 1864.
[66] Mary Eugenia Suter, *Memories of Yesteryear: A History of the Suter Family* (Waynesboro, VA: Charles F. McClung, Printer Inc., 1959), 43 cited in Rebecca Suter Lindsay, "Emanuel Suter Family: Refugees Sent North," *Shenandoah Mennonite Historian* 22, no. 4 (2014): 7.
[67] Suter Diary, 4,5 as quoted in Lindsay, "Emanuel Suter Family," 7.
[68] Michael Shank to Brother Funk, November 19, 1864, published in *Herald of Truth*, December 1864.

October.⁶⁹ Departure dates are not known for Dunkers John and Rebecca Bowman and the various members of their extended family. They "fled with Sheridan's wagon train to the north and on to Ohio until the war was over."⁷⁰

The movement of the refugees was noted in both the Southern and Northern press reflecting regional biases. In Richmond, passengers arriving from the Valley gave accounts of the "havoc committed by the enemy in the vicinity of Harrisonburg and below." After a brief description of the burning and destruction which left the country "a waste," the article added, "It is said that about two hundred Dutch families went off with the Yankees this trip, bag and baggage from Rockingham County. They were a worthless part of the population, and burned their houses and barns before leaving."⁷¹ A more sympathetic report appeared a few days later in a Wheeling, West Virginia, newspaper:

> *Another lot of refugees from the Valley arrived in the city yesterday en route for Ohio. In all, eight hundred families have been shipped from the Valley at government expense by order of Gen. Sheridan. The most of them belong to the society of Dunkarths, and being opposed to taking up arms they have been terribly persecuted by the rebels. They are a hardy looking set of men, who will be an important accession to any Northern community.*⁷²

In his *Personal Memoirs*, General Sheridan does not mention wagons filled with refugees. He does offer his thoughts about war and the relationship between men killing men and "the material interests" that seem to lie beyond the battlefield. He believed that war was too easy for those "who rest at home in peace and plenty" but "see little of the horrors." It was necessary, he reasoned, that "deprivation and suffering" be "brought to their own doors." He contended that loss of material goods was greater "punishment" than death, and concluded "reduction to poverty brings prayers for

---

⁶⁹ D.H. Landis to Daniel Brenneman, October 30, 1864, published in *Herald of Truth*, December 1864.
⁷⁰ Rodes and Wenger, eds., *Unionists*, 5: 578.
⁷¹ *Daily Dispatch* (Richmond, VA), October 11, 1864.
⁷² *The Wheeling Daily Intelligencer*, October 17, 1864.

peace more surely and more quickly than does the destruction of human life."[73]

General Sheridan may have chosen not to remember those "400 or more wagons." But those who offered fervent prayers for peace long before his arrival in the Shenandoah Valley, in the face of multi-faceted persecution and deprivation, sought to hold fast to religious convictions and loyalty to their government. Those who had endured "bonds, imprisonment, and even death," those men, women, children, and their descendants, would remember the fiery autumn of 1864 when they went north with Sheridan's wagon trains.

---

[73] Sheridan, *Personal Memoirs*, 1: 488.

Judge Richard Parker's Loyalty
The Parker-Imboden Correspondence, Spring 1864

Trish Ridgeway

Judge Richard Parker was frustrated and angry. He was well regarded in his hometown of Winchester and in the Commonwealth of Virginia. Confederate president Jefferson Davis as well as many members of Davis' cabinet, knew him. Parker had relatives who held senior posts in the Confederate military.[1] How could anyone doubt his allegiance to the Confederate cause? But they did.

On Friday, April 22, 1864, the fifty-three-year-old Parker reached a Confederate military outpost in Woodstock, Virginia, on his way home to Winchester from Richmond. As he prepared to leave the next day, he was stopped and did not reach home until the following Tuesday. Parker told the outpost's commander, Captain Thomas Davis, who was a Maryland native, that as a Marylander Davis might not know him.[2] Davis replied that they did know him, and that is why Parker was stopped.[3]

Five years prior, Parker achieved fame as the judge who presided over the trial of John Brown and sentenced him to death in the autumn of 1859. During the war, Parker lived in Winchester, occasionally performing judicial duties during Confederate occupations of the town. He kept a diary during the war that had

---

[1] Richard Parker Diary, 1862-1864, June 29-July 10, 1863. Library of Congress, Washington, D.C. (Transcribed by Trish Ridgeway), accessed June 1, 2019, https://lccn.loc.gov/mm94006311. Hereafter cited as LOC.
[2] Captain Thomas Sturgis Davis (1836-1883) described enemy movements from an outpost in Woodstock in an April 8, 1864, report to Brigadier General John D. Imboden. *O.R.*, ser. 1, vol. 51, pt. 2, 853.
[3] A letter from Judge Richard Parker to Brigadier General John D. Imboden, April 28, 1864, (transcribed by Trish Ridgeway) describes in detail the events at the Woodstock outpost. Parker's letter and Imboden's May 2, 1864, reply to Parker are found in the Judge Richard Parker Papers, folder 3, Chicago History Museum, Chicago, IL. Hereafter cited as CHM.

brief entries. In his diary, he wrote that he left Winchester for Richmond on April 13, 1864. Confederate troops arrived in the city the previous day; therefore, Parker did not need a pass to leave. After dropping off relatives in Harrisonburg, Parker arrived in Richmond three days later. He obtained a pass in Staunton for the Woodstock outpost. In his diary, he made slight mention of the difficulties of his April 1864 return trip: "Left for home, Friday [April 22] night. Got to Woodstock in stage. . . . Next morning Captain Davis (of Maryland) in whose company Jim Riely is a 3^d Lieutenant, refused me leave to pass this outpost.[4] Got home Tuesday morning late."[5]

The diary contains scant details of the encounter. However, Parker described the incident in full in a six-page, April 28, 1864, letter he wrote to the outpost's commander, Brigadier General John D. Imboden.[6] He continued his dialogue with Davis on Sunday, April 24, and the charges Davis made are part of the letter:

> *I wished to know the charges against me & also who were my accusers. He said there were no accusers & that he had acted on general rumours.*
>
> *Having reason to think there were one or more about him, who had suggested this procedure as regards me, I pressed this matter further, but he most emphatically repeated that there was no accuser.*
>
> *To further inquiries from me, he specified that I had never before since the first occupation of Winchester by the enemy been inside of (the Confederate) lines, to which I replied I had on two occasions, once (last July) to attend a District Court at Charlottesville, being the only time that public duty called on me to do so: that we, who had*

---

[4] James Purvis Riely (abt.1840-abt. 1887) was a Winchester native and son of James Purvis Riely, Sr. (1808-1860), who was a lawyer and member of the local judicial bar with Parker. Second Lieutenant James P. Riely served with the 23rd Virginia Cavalry.
[5] Richard Parker, Diary, April [28], 1864, LOC.
[6] Brigadier General John D. Imboden, 1823-1895, commanded a variety of Confederate forces in the Valley, including cavalry, mounted infantry, infantry, horse artillery, and partisan rangers. Richard Parker to Brigadier General John D. Imboden, April 28, 1864, CHM.

remained in Winchester had well considered the matter in advance, & that I yet thought I had done right in remaining: but that this could be inquired into.

Then that I had never been molested by the Yankees: that nearly every prominent citizen of Winchester except myself had been arrested whilst they, & especially Milroy commanded it.[7] I denied that any such distinction had been made between me and others--certainly, none such has been made at my instance. That if I had not been arrested then, neither, I believe, during that time have Mr. Conrad, Dr. Boyd, Mr. Williams, Mr. Barton, Mr. Graham, Mr. Holliday, Dr. Conrad, Mr. Meade or: that in property I had suffered like most others, but that all this could likewise be inquired into.[8]

He then expressed some surprise I had not been arrested lately, as one of the hostages for the Morgan County arrests.[9] I said I had heard that my name was upon the list of those to be seized but that I had been taken off at the request of one who claims to hold my office under either

---

[7] Robert Huston Milroy (1816-1890) was a lawyer and judge prior to the war. As a Union general, he commanded the federal occupying forces from January 1, 1863, until his defeat at the 2nd Battle of Winchester, June 13-15, 1863.

[8] Although Parker does not provide first names, these men were in Winchester at the time: Robert Young Conrad, 1805-1875, a lawyer who represented Winchester and Frederick County at the Virginia Secession Convention; Rev. Andrew Hunter Holmes Boyd, 1814-1865, a Presbyterian minister; Philip Williams, 1802-1868, a lawyer in partnership with David W. Barton, David Walker Barton, 1801-1863, was deceased by this time, but Parker may have mentioned him anyway; Dr. James Robert Graham, 1824-1914, a Presbyterian minister; General Thomas Jonathan "Stonewall" Jackson and his wife lived in the Graham home from 1861 to 1862; Robert B. Holliday, 1809-1893, banker; Dr. Daniel Burr Conrad, 1831-1898, was a cousin of Parker's wife, Evelina (Conrad was a surgeon with the Confederate Navy). Parker specifically identifies him later in the letter; therefore, he was in Winchester at this time. Nathaniel Burwell Meade, 1828-1888, is listed in 1870 census with the occupation of editor.

[9] On March 19, 1864, Colonel Charles T. Ferrall, 1840-1905, with the 23rd Virginia Cavalry led a raid on a "Union League" meeting in Bath, now Berkley Springs, Morgan County, WV. They captured several civilians, including two members of the "bogus" Virginia Legislature, two Union soldiers and many horses. Dispatch from Lieutenant John Robert Nunn, Provost Marshal's Office, Harrisonburg, March 29, 1864, to Brigadier General John D. Imboden, *O.R.*, ser. 2, vol. 6, pt. 1, 1120.

the Pierpoint or the W. Va. Government (and on the hearing the next day this appeared probable such a statement having come to us from two entirely different directions).[10]

Again, he said I had not been required like others to take the oath of allegiance. As our people had never so far as I have heard been required to take such an oath, except when they were asking some privilege of or making some complaint to their military, I assumed he meant a parole, which Gen. White, when in command here, had determined to enact; and so understanding him, I reflect that I had not a doubt I almost knew, it would have been exacted of me, but that Gen. White had been compelled to evacuate the town before he could enforce this order save in a few instances: but this also could be inquired into.[11]

He further referred to the action of the Va. Legislature in raising the pay of some of our judges, the bill not including me, as evidence that I was not regarded as loyal to her. To which I answered that from what I had heard of the action of the Legislature I had drawn a very different inference; but that fortunately Mr. Moses Walton, a member of that body was a citizen of Woodstock, & his testimony could be easily obtained.[12]

---

[10] Francis Harrison Pierpont, 1814-1899, elected governor of the Restored Government of Virginia, June 11, 1861, which was comprised of the counties of Virginia, now West Virginia, that remained loyal to the Union. When West Virginia became a state on June 20, 1863, Pierpont continued as governor of Virginia (the Union-occupied territories).

[11] General Julius White, 1816-1870, commanded the Union Eighth Corps that occupied Winchester from July 30, 1862, to September 2, 1862. He refused passes to residents to leave town unless they took the oath of allegiance, and some residents feared imprisonment or banishment if they did not take the oath. Some leading citizens did take a negotiated, modified oath or parole (Barton, Williams, Boyd and Graham) while others, such as Robert Y. Conrad, refused. Eloise C. Strader, ed., *The Civil War Journal of Mary Greenhow Lee* (Winchester, VA: Winchester-Frederick County Historical Society, 2001), 119, 131-134.

[12] The Virginia General Assembly passed an act on December 16, 1863, increasing the salaries of "judges of the circuit courts not residing with the lines of the enemy." *Acts of the General Assembly of the State of Virginia, Passed at the Called Session of 1863* (Richmond: Ritchie, 1863), 26. Moses Walton, 1826-1883, was a lawyer who served in the Virginia House of Delegates, representing the Shenandoah district, from September 7, 1863, to the end of the war.

I told him I had made these inquiries so that I might know what witnesses to produce; that I would then necessarily have to obtain them from Winchester, because well as I was known in Woodstock, its gentlemen could not speak of their own knowledge as to my course in Winchester: that I invited the strictest scrutiny as to my course from the beginning of the war & was sure no man of character in my town could be found, who would say one word which could incur my detention.

He then told me he had also military reasons for not letting me pass the day before, & he had left orders for a passport to be given me the following day. To which I remarked that he had permitted others to pass through his pickets on Saturday, & that I did not think I could accept a passport now, without an open investigation into my whole conduct.[13]

Captain Davis appeared to have lost interest in detaining Parker, and the captain left Woodstock the next day, but Parker was determined to pursue a vigorous defense of his reputation before some military official. He sent a letter to Winchester friends on Sunday, and his witnesses appeared on Monday:

About midday of Monday (the 25th) in consequences of my note, Dr. Daniel Conrad & Mr. N.B. Meade arrived, & soon after I went into the military office, where I found Major Calmese in command,[14] mentioned my having asked on the previous Saturday permission to pass the Outposts but that it had been refused me; inquiries if any charges had been left with regard to me, and was told there were none.

I then recapitulated, as faithfully as I could, the reasons I have before made mention of assigned by Capt. Davis for

---

[13] Richard Parker to Brigadier General John D. Imboden, April 28, 1864, CHM.
[14] Major Fielding H. Calmese, 1832-1901, was a Clarke County, Virginia, resident who served in the 23rd Virginia Cavalry under Imboden.

his refusal; that I very much regretted the Captain's absence, but these gentlemen said it would incommode them greatly to be detained longer than was necessary; & that as I had been openly refused a passport for these reasons, I was ready to show how unjustly I had been treated & would do so openly by these my witnesses & if their testimony was such as to authorize it, I should then renew my application to pass through the outposts.

I examined Mr. Walton & Mr. Meade, the later very closely and fully; I insisted & urged that any & every inquiry, that could be suggested, be put to them. The testimony I will not detail, it covered all the grounds alleged, & many other matters not alluded to by the Captain, tending to show my real position throughout. It is enough for me to say I had no reason to regret the investigation; perhaps a report has been made to you by Major Calmese in regard to it. Dr. Conrad tho not examined particularly; it being deemed a waste of time to do so, took occasion to express his sense & that of others, at the treatment I had been subjected to. They also presented & left a paper, got up in Winchester, as soon as my detention was known, & signed as they asserted, by every one to whom there was time to present it.[15]

Major Fielding Calmese signed the pass and the group left on Monday, reaching Winchester on Tuesday. Parker informed Imboden that he had previously heard tales about his allegiance to the Confederacy: "I have before heard of these slanderous rumours respecting myself & others, but I have hitherto treated them with the contempt I thought they merited. I knew they could proceed from none but the lowest sources, and I did not believe there was an honest-hearted gentleman in the State, who could be imposed upon by them."[16]

Brigadier General John D. Imboden wrote a reply to Parker's letter on May 2, 1864.[17] Imboden stated that he had paid little

---

[15] Richard Parker to Brigadier General John D. Imboden, April 28, 1864, CHM.
[16] Ibid.
[17] Letter from Brigadier General John D. Imboden to Judge Richard Parker, May 2, 1864, (transcribed by Trish Ridgeway), Judge Richard Parker Papers, folder 3, CHM.

attention when handed a telegram from Parker on April 23, "being very busy at the time." Imboden was commanding Confederate forces in the Valley. His scouts had informed him of Union General Franz Sigel's movements. Sigel had gathered his troops in Martinsburg by March 25, with orders to move south. Siegel arrived in Winchester on April 30.

Imboden told Parker that had Parker signed the telegraph with Judge Richard Parker he would have immediately sent word for Parker to pass through the lines, but he did not realize who Parker was and assumed that Captain Davis was following orders:

> *I have not seen Capt. Davis nor heard from him on this subject. I cannot conceive of any motive on <u>his</u> part to do otherwise than faithfully discharge his official duty. I cannot attribute to him any feeling of <u>spite</u>, knowing him as well as I do as a high bred gentleman, and a faithful and intelligent officer. That he had really heard about you whatever he alleged, I cannot doubt, for as a truthful gentleman he would not have professed to have heard things, which were only inventions of his own.*
>
> *And it is due that I should say further in defense of Capt. Davis that painful rumours in regard to your position and feelings in this revolution have been in circulation for some time. By whom originated & circulated, or on what alleged information I cannot tell, for I do not remember the name of anyone I ever heard speak on the subject, and yet I know that I have frequently heard the matter discussed or referred to up and down the Valley. But no <u>facts</u> have ever come to my knowledge that would have caused <u>me</u> to have withheld from you permission to pass the outpost when any other citizen was permitted to go through to his home. Indeed, you state in your letter that you had previously heard of such reports yourself.*[18]

Imboden concluded his letter by assuring Parker that Parker's letter would be held in the files of the headquarters as the

---

[18] Brigadier General John D. Imboden to Richard Parker, May 2, 1864, CHM.

judge had requested.

Both Parker and Imboden seem to have concluded the incident stemmed from rumors about Parker's allegiance to the Confederate cause. Officials in areas under one command during the war greatly feared spies and saboteurs and valued gossip about those with subversive opinions. For instance, the Richmond city council passed a law that told citizens it was their duty to inform the mayor of anyone suspected of "entertaining or having expressed sentiments that render such person suspicious."[19] Baltimore was under Union control throughout the war but had an active community of secessionists in its population. Federal authorities there received so much frivolous gossip about suspected Confederates that they required informants to provide their accusations in writing with full details.[20]

Since control of Winchester changed frequently from one opposing army to another, residents on both sides knew not to count on their army staying in control for too long. Supporters of either side were reluctant to become publicly known as an informant. Most of the information that circulated about Judge Parker during the Civil War is lost to history, but there are a few documents, both formal and informal, that cast light on his leanings or report there were rumors.

Parker attended law classes at the University of Virginia and returned to Berryville to practice law in 1833. Judge Richard Elliott Parker, Richard Parker's father, died in 1840 and left him "The Retreat" in what is now Clarke County. In the 1830 slave census, Richard Elliott owned twenty-three slaves in the Eastern District of Frederick County.[21] In the 1860 Winchester Slave Census, Richard Parker is listed as the owner of nine slaves.[22]

He served as the Military Storekeeper and Paymaster of the United States Armory and Arsenal at Harpers Ferry from 1838-1847 when he left to resume his law practice. In 1848, Richard Parker

---

[19] Louis H. Manarin, ed., *Richmond at War: The Minutes of the City Council 1861-1865* (Chapel Hill: University of North Carolina Press, 1966), 30-31.
[20] Major General John Wool, General Orders, No. 30, Baltimore, Sept. 1, 1862. O.R., ser. 1, vol. 19, pt. 2, 286-7.
[21] U.S. Census Bureau, 1830 United States Census, Eastern District, Frederick, Virginia, M19, roll 190, 77.
[22] U.S. Census Bureau, 1860 United States Census, Slave Schedules, Winchester, Frederick County, M653.

returned home to Berryville from Charles Town and opened a law office there.

He took a case to trial on May 16, 1849, that must have had the citizens of Berryville and Winchester buzzing. He represented Judith in the case of *Bennett Russell and Others vs. Negroes Judith and Others*. John Russell Crafton (sometime in his life he dropped the Crafton) died in 1848. He stipulated in his 1839 will that his slaves be freed upon his death. His son, Bennett Russell, and siblings produced an 1842 Articles of Agreement that retracted the manumission. There is doubt about the authenticity of the articles. Parker represented Judith in the 1849 trial that ended with a hung jury and in the second trial in 1850 that also ended in a hung jury. When the case went to trial again in 1856, Parker had become a judge and could no longer serve as legal counsel in the case. The 1856 verdict was in favor of the heirs, and the slaves were sold.[23]

Richard Parker was elected to the U.S. House of Representatives and served from March 4, 1849, to March 3, 1851, when he was appointed a judge to the general court in the Winchester and Frederick County area. While in Congress on February 23, 1850, he made a speech on the question of admitting California as a free or slave-holding state. He used legal arguments in discussing the wrongs that Northern states had committed against their Southern counterparts and listed the grievances:

- In Northern states, the reluctance to enforce the law and the sometimes violence toward slave catchers who were attempting to retrieve "fugitives from labor" [Parker's term] and return the slaves to the South,
- The insistence by the North that they could legislate to exclude slavery from the territories, and
- The attempts by the North to encroach on the rights of slave-holding states although the Constitution recognized the right to own slaves.

---

[23] Jesse Russell II Collection., 928 THL, Stewart Bell, Jr. Archives, Handley Regional Library, Winchester, VA; and Jesse L. Russell, *Juliet, from Slavery to Inspiration* (Self-published, 2018).

Parker concluded his speech with a warning to the North:

> *I trust, that before this session closes, many northern representatives in this chamber will, for the sake of peace and to preserve the Union, range themselves with us under the only banner beneath which confederated republics can safely form, the banner of Equality of right, and of the Abstinence from exercise of doubtful powers... But should I be disappointed in this hope—should aggression be accumulated upon aggression, and wrong against wrong—it is not for me to predict what line of conduct Virginia will pursue. That is not within the province of any of her representatives here. That she will determine for herself in convention of her people, and that determination once made will be binding upon all her sons.*[24]

Judge Richard Parker was a name that became well-known to the people throughout the nation who were following the trial of John Brown in their local newspapers. Parker happened to be the circuit court judge assigned to hear cases in the county seat of Charles Town, Virginia (now West Virginia) when John Brown and his raiders were arrested. There is no documentary evidence that any Confederates thought his handling of the trial revealed Unionist leanings—he did sentence Brown to death.

Parker and others wanted to ensure that Northerners viewed the trial as fair, and Parker strictly adhered to Virginia law during the trial. The law gave Brown the right to speak before sentencing, and Brown gave an impassioned speech that was widely reprinted. Virginia law mandated time for appeal after sentencing, and Parker specified one month between sentencing and execution, time that Brown used to send out many letters that were published in the Northern press. Although Northerners felt Parker had rushed the trial, he also unwittingly gave Brown the platform that transformed Osawatomie Brown from murderer to martyr in the eyes of many

---

[24] *Hon. Richard Parker of Virginia, President's Message in Relation to California, Delivered in the House of Representative, Thursday, February 23, 1850* (Washington, D.C.: Congressional Globe Office, 1850), 8.

Northerners.[25]

In his letter to Imboden, Parker stated that he had heard that his name had been removed, either by the Francis Pierpont or the West Virginia Government, from the list of men to be arrested. Others probably heard the same report—such favoritism from a Unionist certainly would have led to speculation about Parker's loyalty. His relationship with Pierpont is unclear. Pierpont was governor of the Restored Government of Virginia in 1864, governing from federally-controlled Alexandria and moving to Richmond at the conclusion of the war. Pierpont received an April 24, 1862, letter from Christopher L. Grafflin from Morgan County:

> *Our Court will meet next Monday, and immediately afterwards I will be able to send you a correct list of Loyal & Disloyal officers of our County—and we have determined to hold the Election at the usual time in May. The 6th of May is the usual time for holding our Circuit Court. We have not heard from Judge Parker, but have reason to think he is Loyal; and if so, would be glad to have him resume his duties, he being very acceptable to the people.*[26]

Although Parker did not assume a judgeship in the restored government, he was viewed, at least by some, as probably loyal. After the war Pierpont appointed Parker as a judge and assigned him the task of restructuring the courts and the civil government in Parker's former circuit.[27]

---

[25] A detailed analysis of the trial is found in Brian McGinty, *John Brown's Trial* (Cambridge: Harvard University Press, 2009). A full discussion of the influence of the raid and trial is provided by John Stauffer and Zoe Trodd, eds., *The Tribunal: Responses to John Brown and the Harpers Ferry Raid* (Cambridge: Belknap Press, Harvard University, 2012).

[26] Christopher L. Grafflin, 1823-1887, enlisted in the Union army September 2, 1862. C. L. Grafflin, letter to F.H. Pierpont, April 24, 1862. Pierpont-Samuels Collection, Ar1722, West Virginia State Archives, Charleston, WV.

[27] Boyd B. Stutler, "Judge Richard Parker—He Tried John Brown," *Magazine of the Jefferson County Historical Society* 19 (December 1953): 36. In an August 19, 1865, entry in his memorandum book, page c, Parker notes, "Qualified before Jos. S. Denny J. P. to commission from Govr. Pierpoint." Richard Parker, Memorandum Book pertaining to business in other counties than Jefferson, John Brown/Boyd B. Stutler Collection Database, West Virginia Department of Arts, Culture and History, item 955, accessed June 1, 2019, www.wvculture.org/history/wvmemory/jbdetail.aspx?Type=Text&Id=955; Joseph S. Denny, 1825-1899, was a justice of the peace in Frederick County, Virginia.

John Peyton Clark, who was principal of the Winchester Academy before it closed in 1861, discussed the appointment of judges in an April 24, 1862, journal entry. He said it came about through officials of the Pierpont dynasty, "endeavoring to organize the courts and establish the reign of civil law" while Winchester was under Union control. Three magistrates took an oath of allegiance, according to Clark

> *all of whom, either from cowardice, ignorance, or inclination, took it without protest or remonstrance... Judge Parker, as well as I can understand him, may be termed non-committal. He emphasizes the importance of civil law, and whilst I heard him repudiate the idea of an oath or any action under the Pierpont Government on the part of magistrates and other officers, yet I fear he may be not as decided in his intercourse with them. I see him often in much closer intercourse with some of them than, according to my ideas, is neither becoming or patriotic.*[28]

Parker was friends with David Hunter Strother, "Porte Crayon," before the war and attended his wedding in Charles Town on May 6, 1861. Strother joined the Union army in March 1862 and received a commission from Pierpont as a lieutenant colonel of the 3rd West Virginia Cavalry in June 1862. Strother was on General Franz Sigel's staff in spring 1864. Strother, a Valley native was reviled in the Shenandoah as a traitor.[29] Since Sigel's forces threatened Winchester at the time Parker was stopped in Woodstock, his affiliation with Strother might have been a military reason for delaying Parker's return to Winchester. Strother was also a friend of Pierpont and came with him to Richmond in 1865 to serve in the new government.

The discussions about Parker that arose in the Virginia General Assembly when it discussed a pay raise for judges also cast light on the rumors about Parker. James Dillon Armstrong, a loyal

---

[28] John Peyton Clark Journal, April 24, 1862, Louisa Morrow Crawford Collection, Stewart Bell, Jr. Archives, Handley Regional Library, Winchester, VA.
[29] David Hunter Strother, 1816-1888, was a well-known artist and writer before and after the war. For additional discussion see Cecil D. Eby, Jr., *"Port Crayon": The Life of David Hunter Strother* (Westport, CT: Greenwood, 1960), 107, 114, 157-159.

Confederate who represented Hampshire, Hardy, and Morgan counties in the Virginia Senate, wrote Parker on November 3, 1863. Armstrong stated that the Senate was considering a bill that had been passed by the House. The bill raised the pay of judges in the state who were not in Union-occupied territories. House member George William Ward, who represented Winchester, proposed a rider that was approved, by the House, to include Parker in the group to receive raises.

In the Senate debate, Senator John Brannon moved to strike the rider

> *on the grounds as at first stated that it would be sanctioning your loyalty and that he could not do as there were rumours that you were disloyal. Before the discussion was through, he explained that he did not mean to charge you with being disloyal but that he understood you had occupied an equivocal position that you had not taken the bold and decisive stance that one holding the office you did, should have done and that he did not know why it was that you could remain unmolested in the Yankee lines which all other officers had either been arrested or compelled to flee & that your position needed explanation.*[30]

Why was Parker not detained while Union forces arrested other notable Winchester residents? Parker was wrong in his statement to Captain Davis that no one he had listed had been previously arrested. Robert Y. Conrad was arrested and briefly held August 29, 1863, and others were also arrested and briefly held.[31] Conrad was again arrested on January 19, 1864, in retaliation for the arrest of William Dooley by Confederate forces, but was

---

[30] James Dillon Armstrong to Judge Richard Parker, November 3, 1863, (transcribed by Trish Ridgeway), Judge Richard Parker Papers, folder 3, CHM. The letter lacks direct indication that it is addressed to Parker, but its contents indicate that it was sent to him. James Dillon Armstrong, 1821-1893, represented Hampshire, Hardy and Morgan counties in the Virginia Senate. John Brannon represented the counties, now in West Virginia, of Lewis, Barbour, Upshur, Gilmer, Randolph, Tucker, and part of Webster in the Virginia Senate.

[31] Richard R. Duncan, *Beleaguered Winchester: a Virginia Community at War, 1861-1865* (Baton Rouge: Louisiana State University Press, 2007), 119-121.

immediately released.³² Rev. Andrew Boyd was also arrested, on January 23, 1864, in retaliation for the Dooley incident. Boyd was taken to Martinsburg, returned home four days later, paroled and ordered to report to authorities every ten days.³³

On April 4, Boyd, Williams, and Conrad were taken as hostages for the men captured at Bath, what Captain Davis called the Morgan County arrests. Federal troops took the three men to Martinsburg, where they were imprisoned. Conrad was released on April 23 and given sixty days, according to Laura Lee's diary, to go to Richmond to "arrange an exchange with those miserable scamps for whom they were held."³⁴ These arrests were made less than three weeks before Parker arrived at the Woodstock outpost, and Parker uses the three men as references in his discussion with Captain Davis.

Despite his John Brown fame, Parker may not have been as well-known to Union troops as the men who were jailed. As stated above, Brannon in the Virginia Senate debate stated Parker did not take a "bold and decisive stance." The words and actions of others in town probably attracted more federal attention. Although Mary Greenhow Lee felt Philip Williams was too timid in his dealings with federal officials, she recorded five instances before April 23 when he appealed directly to Union authorities on behalf of local citizens.³⁵

Dr. Boyd preached his Confederate sympathies from the pulpit. Julia Chase, a Union supporter who attended his church, stated that Boyd, "said in a sermon preached on the 18th of September [1862], a day appointed by Jeff Davis as a day of prayer and thanksgiving, that God was certainly on the side of the South, because they were a praying people... that the North were not a praying or religious people."³⁶

---

[32] Michael G. Mahon, ed., *Winchester Divided: The Civil War Diaries of Julia Chase and Laura Lee* (Mechanicsburg, PA: Stackpole, 2002), 130.
[33] Report to Headquarters, 3rd Brigade, 1st Division, Dept. of West Virginia, from Captain W.M. Boone, O.R., ser. 1, vol. 33, 409; Strader, ed., *The Civil War Journal*, 328.
[34] Mahon, ed., *Winchester Divided*, 139-140.
[35] Strader, ed., *The Civil War Journal*, 128. Instances of Williams appealing to federal forces: 34, 131, 215, 303.
[36] Julia Chase Diary, September 23, 1862, Julia Chase Collection, Stewart Bell, Jr. Archives, Handley Regional Library, Winchester, VA, quoted in Garland R. Quarles, *Occupied Winchester, 1861-1865* (Winchester, VA: Farmers & Merchants National Bank, 1976), 114.

Robert Conrad was a leader of the pro-Union supporters in the 1861 Virginia Convention that eventually voted to secede, but he did throw his support to the Confederate cause after voting no to secession. He refused to take the Union's modified oath of allegiance or parole that Williams and Boyd had signed. Mrs. Lee recorded several instances that Conrad stood up to Union troops and thought that "He is the only one in Winchester, whose conduct to the Yankees, from the beginning of the war, has met with my unqualified approbation."[37]

Parker does not show up in Mary Greenhow Lee's diary as interacting with Union soldiers. He stated in his January 1, 1863, diary entry after Milroy arrived in Winchester, "Genl. Milroy himself, with a number of troops, arrived about midday. The number I do not know. In such times I stay almost entirely at home."[38] Parker did write a letter to Milroy asking that Washington G. Singleton, the clerk of both the circuit court and district court of appeals, not be removed from his house.[39] Parker undoubtedly had a strong connection with this officer of the court.

Mary Greenhow Lee's judgment of Parker, written in a June 16, 1864, journal entry, casts some light on earlier rumors about him, "How he has changed; at the commencement of the war we barely spoke, on account of his Union proclivities; now he is a good Southerner."[40]

In a diary entry on July 24, 1864, Parker showed antipathy to the Union army: "Each new advance of the foe into our town increases our alarms: for the war is becoming one of oppression & outrage upon the citizens under the pretext of retaliation."[41] Parker and other Winchester citizens had endured three major Union occupations as well as the First and Second Battles of Winchester, along with other smaller actions. Union troops had been raiding and riding through Winchester for the last year. There had been numerous arrests of Confederate citizens in retaliation for the actions of the Confederate army. His choice of the word "becoming" makes one wonder if his sentiments *had* seen a change. Or was the

---

[37] Strader, ed., *The Civil War Journal*, 326.
[38] Richard Parker Diary, January 1, 1863, LOC.
[39] General Robert H. Milroy to Judge Richard Parker, May 30, 1863, Judge Richard Parker Papers, folder 3, CHM.
[40] Strader, ed., *The Civil War Journal*, 371.
[41] Richard Parker Diary, July 24, 1864, LOC.

verb simply a bad choice in a hastily written diary entry?

Parker's references to the oaths of office required by Union officials made the requirement seem a minor problem. Jonathan M. Berkey in his excellent essay, "Swallowing the Oath, the Battle over Citizenship in Occupied Winchester," illustrates that the refusal to take the oath, especially during earlier Union occupations, severely limited civilians' abilities to move freely and to locate food and other necessities. He concludes that Winchester's Confederate supporters were unified and strengthened by their communal bonds.[42]

Richard Parker, although he may have had doubts about secession, was bound to the Winchester and Clarke County community by many family and professional ties. When his loyalty was questioned, that community sent two of their leaders to support him, and they carried a document signed by others.

Judge Parker was a man of the law. He probably did not want Virginia to break its constitutional bond with the Union. As shown in his speech before Congress, he shared Robert Conrad's conviction that the people of the North would not allow a schism to come. A review of the documentary evidence concerning his allegiance to the Confederate cause gives no unequivocal answer except that some had grave doubts about him. Unionists too hoped his reputation meant he was on their side. He probably said much more on the subject, but it seems all other records and gossip are lost to history. Mary Greenhow Lee believed Parker had evolved into a "good Southerner," but does not tell us why.

Parker's letter to Imboden illustrates how strong his lawyerly instincts were as he described examining witnesses and then insisting his letter be maintained in Imboden's official files. He could not, however, fully defend himself against accusations of disloyalty. Both he and Imboden recognized the perils of maintaining a good name in a land torn by war where individuals that staunchly adhered to the Confederacy would not forget or forgive real or imagined treacherous words or deeds.

---

[42] Jonathan M. Berkey, "Swallowing the Oath: The Battle Over Citizenship in Occupied Winchester" in Paul Quigley, ed., *The Civil War and the Transformation of American Citizenship* (Baton Rouge: Louisiana State Press, 2018), 89-112.

Book Reviews

Reexamining *The Stonewall Brigade*

The Stonewall Brigade by James I. Robertson, Jr. Baton Rouge: Louisiana State University Press, 1963. ISBN: 978-08-07107171.

Review by Jonathan M. Berkey

The Civil War centennial witnessed the publication of scholarly studies of two of the conflict's most famous brigades. Two years after the appearance of Alan T. Nolan's *The Iron Brigade: A Military History* (1961), Louisiana State University Press released James I. Robertson, Jr.'s study of the Stonewall Brigade. Robertson's work offers a brisk narrative of the brigade's history from its formation at Harpers Ferry in the spring of 1861 through its decimation at the battle of Spotsylvania in 1864.

The Stonewall Brigade, comprised of five regiments organized throughout the Shenandoah Valley, fought in thirty-nine engagements during the war. On May 30, 1863 the Confederate government approved the petition of brigade officers to have the unit officially designated as the Stonewall Brigade. It was the only brigade in the Confederate military to have an official nickname.

The early chapters of *The Stonewall Brigade* reflect the priorities and style of Robertson's mentor Bell Wiley. Robertson argues that several factors contributed to the evolution of a mass of undisciplined Virginia recruits into a cohesive and effective fighting force. Early chapters explain that common ethnic backgrounds and kinship ties helped the Valley men forge a strong sense of identity.

The brigade's relationship to its first commander and namesake overshadowed these cohesive factors. Robertson notes that after a rough start, Thomas Jonathan Jackson soon became a source of inspiration and pride to his men. Jackson's quiet confidence, earnestness, and his zeal for victory made him popular among the brigade's soldiers. A string of remarkable victories, beginning with the first battle of Manassas—where the brigade and its leader earned their famous nicknames—greatly eased this bonding process.

The Stonewall Brigade's speed and endurance exhibited during the 1862 Valley campaign earned the men a second nickname: Jackson's "foot cavalry." Fifty minutes of rapid marching followed by ten minutes of rest characterized many of the brigade's movements in the Valley. This pace allowed Jackson's men to cover twenty-six miles in the Luray Valley to reach Front Royal in sixteen hours on May 23, 1862, initiating the Confederate turn of fortune in the 1862 Valley campaign. Robertson notes that the brigade completed similar feverish-paced marches in many campaigns outside of the Valley.

That the Stonewall Brigade could march at such a pace and remain an effective fighting force is a testament to its commanders. Robertson effectively chronicles the generally tragic careers of the brigade's leaders. Each commander endured a period of tension with the Valley soldiers before earning their trust. For instance, the arrest of his predecessor, Richard B. Garnett, caused Brigadier General Charles S. Winder's first weeks of command to be a challenge. Many Valley soldiers disapproved of Garnett's treatment and refused to cheer or acknowledge Winder when he came into their presence. That Winder was from Maryland did not help his cause in the Virginia brigade. Major Frank Paxton faced similar displeasure when he was chosen to lead the brigade over Colonel Andrew J. Grigsby, who was the ranking officer in the brigade and had led it after the death of Winder at Cedar Mountain. When Colonel James A. Walker assumed command following Paxton's demise at Chancellorsville, all five regimental commanders resigned in protest (Robert E. Lee persuaded the officers to stay with the brigade and its new leader). In all of these cases, the men and their officers warmed up to their commanders with time.

As his analysis of commanders shows, Robertson does not shy away from discussing less-flattering aspects of the Stonewall Brigade. He observes that the soldiers' confidence at times bordered on cockiness, which made discipline a challenge. Instances of desertion and war weariness are discussed along with the military successes of the brigade.

The Stonewall Brigade shows its age in some areas. Robertson deemphasizes slavery's importance to the Valley and its soldiers. Readers hoping to find insights on topics that currently dominate the scholarship on Civil War soldiers—their initial and combat motivation and the psychological effects of battle on them—will be disappointed.

In some ways the greatest strength of Robertson's book is also its most significant weakness. *The Stonewall Brigade*'s fast-paced and entertaining narrative frequently relies on postwar sources. Using these accounts adds drama to the brigade's story, but Robertson does not question evidence that is inclined to mythologize the fallen Jackson and his brigade. Stories of Jackson's fabled piety rubbing off on his soldiers and accounts of dramatic stories of accurate death premonitions by some of the brigade's commanders make for good reading but are not supported by wartime sources.

This caveat aside, *The Stonewall Brigade* provides readers with a well-written introduction to the Valley's—and arguably the Confederacy's—most famous brigade.

Jonathan M. Berkey is professor of history at Concord University in Athens, West Virginia, and the author of various essays and chapters about the Civil War era in the Shenandoah Valley.

At the Forefront of Lee's Invasion: Retribution, Plunder, and Clashing Cultures on Richard S. Ewell's Road to Gettysburg by Robert J. Wynstra. Kent, OH: Kent State University Press, 2018. ISBN: 978-1-60635-354-7.

Review by Barton A. Myers

Robert J. Wynstra's *At the Forefront of Lee's Invasion* offers a careful and well-research examination of General Richard Stoddart Ewell and the Second Corps of the Army of Northern Virginia's raid into the North ahead of the July 1863 Battle of Gettysburg. Upon the death of Stonewall Jackson from pneumonia after being wounded seriously by his own men at the Battle of Chancellorsville, Lee divided Jackson's old command into two corps giving Ambrose Powell Hill the Third Corps and Richard S. Ewell the Second Corps. Throughout 1862, these two officers had proven themselves as two of the best at division level command in the Army of Northern Virginia during their respective performances. Unfortunately, the assessment by many of his men that the arrival in camp of Ewell, minus a leg but with the addition of a wife, did not recreate the whole warrior that had left the army when he was grievously wounded at Groveton in 1862. To quote one soldier who remembered him as a fierce division commander under Jackson, "we were of the opinion that Ewell was not the same soldier he had been when he was a whole man—and a single one." (4) These concerns were shared, at least in part, by General Robert E. Lee himself who was concerned that Ewell quickly moved from "elation to despondency" and sometimes vacillated in decision making. (4) The Second Corps' critical role as a vanguard of the summer 1863 Confederate invasion would, therefore, be an opportunity for Lee to further evaluate Ewell's leadership.

The enormous confiscation and impressment of property, especially cattle and food stuffs, was a huge success of the Confederate military effort in the Cumberland Valley of Pennsylvania, and it was recognized as such by the Confederate War Department. Wynstra's narrative follows Ewell's efforts to impress foodstuffs and other military necessities on the road to Gettysburg. He also addresses the Confederates' capture of hundreds of African-Americans in Pennsylvania, who were then taken back to the South and enslaved. The capture of black Pennsylvanians was sanctioned by Ewell's subordinate commanders, according to Wynstra. (108) If anything, Wynstra might have offered even more analysis of these efforts as part of his overall examination of the clash of regional cultures in this second Southern raid into the North. The Confederates made efforts to pay for many of the supplies impressed and were directly banned on the orders of General Lee from retribution while moving through the Pennsylvania towns. The operations were, nevertheless, terrifying for the Pennsylvanians, who reacted with the logical concern over whether Confederates would burn their towns and sack their cities. Confederates, for their part, were largely controlled in their interactions with civilians, but on rare occasions, individual soldiers, like those in Harry Hay's brigade of "Louisiana Tigers," did commit acts of violence against civilians. (133) In sum, the overall impressment effort was a logistical success for Confederates who needed the supplies. Yet, it was not enough to make up for the devastating defeat and loss of manpower brought about by the three-day engagement at Gettysburg or the subsequent failures of Richard Ewell during the July battle.

Wynstra's book is an engaging read. The volume was thoroughly researched from newspapers and archives drawn from across the United States, a rarity for a work of this focus and specificity in the Civil War field. The book takes on an important topic that has not been researched especially thoroughly, even in the voluminous, and so often repetitive Gettysburg literature. With books like Wynstra's on the bookshelf it opens the possibility of more comparative work on Confederate invasions that might provide new understanding of how Confederate armies handled occupied and captured territory. In short, Wynstra's work reminded me of the best operational military history that originally brought me to the American Civil War in my days as a younger scholar.

Dr. Barton A. Myers is Class of 1960 Associate Professor of Ethics and History Washington and Lee University.

Private Confederacies: The Emotional Worlds of South Men as Citizens and Soldiers by James J. Broomall. Chapel Hill: University of North Carolina Press, 2019. ISBN: 978-1469651989.

Review by Kenneth W. Noe

In the wake of World War II, Bell Wiley published his twin "biographies" of Billy Yank and Johnny Reb. Shaped by postwar military research, Wiley created the modern field of Civil War soldier studies, and his conclusions dominated it for a generation. In the 1980s, a more recent war in Southeast Asia revitalized historians' interests in common soldiers. They filled shelves with books that sought to explain "what they fought for." Countering Wiley's conclusions, many stressed the centrality of political ideology. Some, including this reviewer, made use of representative samples, broad coverage of sources, and statistics. As America's current wars shifted to the Middle East, a new cohort of scholars moved beyond the increasingly well-worn question of motivation to explore other aspects of soldiers' lives, including class, gender, masculinity, and the soldiers' inner lives. Methodologically, most eschew samples and statistics for deep readings of fewer sources.

James J. Broomall's *Private Confederacies* decidedly belongs to the latter school. As his subtitle makes plain, Broomall aims to explain the "emotional worlds of Southern men" before, during, and after the Civil War. Like previous historians, he posits that in the antebellum south, white southern men hid their true selves while trying to conform to society's expectations. Projecting ambition, mastery, and hair-trigger masculinity in public, many of them felt more complex emotions and embarrassing anxieties that they hid from view. Wary of other men, they often confided only in women. Military service cut them off from their homes and forcibly remade their identities. Most men forged new and deep emotional bonds with comrades of the same race, rank, and class. While those ties sustained men in battle, they could not overcome suffering and growing feelings of powerlessness. The randomness and horrors of battlefield death left many confused and vulnerable. The war damaged men irrevocably. When it ended, traumatized veterans found the transition to peace long, hard, and emotional. As Broomall maintains, they *felt* defeat to their cores. In an especially strong chapter, the author explains how some initially acted out, creating more mayhem and violence across the south in 1865 than historians previously recognized. Other veterans banded together to keep the peace, only to increasingly target scapegoated freedpeople. During Reconstruction—another deeply felt experience—bonds between former comrades often grew stronger, as men either rebuilt their lives or sank under the weight of poverty, failure, and despair. Unlike before the war, however, they often turned to each other, benignly at reunions or violently as paramilitaries. Dressed as the ghosts of their doomed comrades risen from Hell, they acted out their impotent rage and hate in thousands of ugly incidents across the region.

Broomall's conclusions are bold and indeed timely. Although he never uses the phrase, his conclusions suggest the widespread existence of what modern observers term "toxic masculinity." The latter half of the book is especially fresh and worthy of discussion. Broomall's decision to carry his soldiers on into the confusion and violence of Reconstruction should serve as a model for others. To be sure, as the author admits, his study of "southern men" largely is an examination of educated slaveholding men from the upper south and Atlantic coast who fought in the Army of Northern Virginia. Nor does Broomall indicate how many soldiers he included in his research, or how many of them deviated from his developing norms. Most chapters rely on the writings of a few individuals. Given my own statistical propensities, I would like to know just how representative they really are. But that ongoing methodological debate aside, *Private Confederacies* deserves a wide readership. It asks new questions and tells us new things about how the Civil War and Reconstruction actually felt.

Kenneth W. Noe is a native of Virginia and currently the Draughon Professor of Southern History at Auburn University. He is most recently the author of Reluctant Rebels: The Confederates Who Joined the Army After 1861 *(2010).*

The War for the Common Soldier: How Men Thought, Fought, and Survived in Civil War Armies by Peter S. Carmichael. Chapel Hill: University of North Carolina Press, 2018. ISBN: 978-1-4696-4309-0.

Review by Jennifer M. Murray

The quest to understand Civil War soldiers is one of the most prevalent endeavors among Civil War scholars. Indeed, the historiography on "common soldiers" is both plentiful and interpretively rich. In general, the scholarship on Civil War soldiers perpetually seeks to understand soldiers' motivations, namely addressing the timeless question of "why did soldiers fight?" Answers to this question often classify soldiers' motivations into an ideological or socio-cultural binary framework. Yet historians' tendencies to scour soldiers' letters for evidence that Union and Confederate soldiers fought for patriotic reasons or enlisted for cultural motivations, obscure the ways in which the soldiers' thoughts and actions were shaped and influenced by their particular circumstance. In *The War for the Common Soldier,* Peter Carmichael, the Robert C. Fluhrer Professor of Civil War Studies at Gettysburg College, complicates the matrix to evaluate Civil War soldiers, their experiences, and their impressions in the nation's bloodiest conflict.

First and foremost, Carmichael disavows the canard of the "common soldier." In seeking to understand the war's "common soldier," Carmichael maintains, "a soldier was never a state of being but always a process in becoming." (9) Focusing on Union and

Confederate soldiers, of both the conflict's eastern and western theaters and exclusively those who saw combat, Carmichael identifies a slate of soldiers whose letters offer the ability to study their wartime experiences over time. Carmichael dives into the entirety of the soldiers' experiences, from camp life to combat to desertion to relations with family members back home, to their understandings of Providence. In doing so, Carmichael presents an analysis of soldiers, not as static actors in a bloody, violent drama, but as men who respond to particular conditions in the fluid environment in which they operated. Central to Carmichael's argument is the belief that Civil War soldiers were pragmatic. Because soldiering was a process, Carmichael believes that these men responded to particular circumstances through "hard-nosed pragmatism." (7)

Case studies provide the framework for the analysis. Joshua Callaway, a soldier in the 28th Alabama, wrote open, emotionally vulnerable letters home to his wife. He commonly referred to himself as a "poor soldier," a description that underscored the hardships of soldier life. Through the language of "poor soldier" or "soldier boy," Carmichael argues for a "soldier consciousness," in which the men portrayed themselves as victims of the army, the state, and the invariably cruel and exacting war. Letters between Captain David Beem, Fourteenth Indiana Infantry, and his wife, Mahala, reveal the complicated relationship between a soldier and a wife, who remained a constant critic of the Union war effort. When Mahala admonished her husband for abandoning her to fight in the Union armies, David launched an assault against her criticism and, in his replies, "became more intransigent in asserting his rights to define duty as he understood it." (112)

In his chapter on religion and Providence, Carmichael advances the historiographic debate by moving the conversation beyond a question of the ways in which soldiers turned to religion to explain battlefield success and defeat. Here again, Carmichael argues that soldiers adopted a pragmatic approach, adapting their religious thinking as conditions dictated. William T. Shepherd of the First Illinois Light Artillery, for example, survived two horrific days of combat at Shiloh in April 1862. His letters reveal that while the battle's horrors haunted him deeply, his experience in combat reinforced his belief in Providence. More than an effort of self-preservation, Carmichael offers, "Shepherd could not allow himself to fall into a depression and become forlorn; he had to repair himself or risk losing God's favor." (96)

In moving beyond the trope of studying *what* soldiers thought, to *how* they thought, and subsequently to how they reacted to these conditions, Carmichael has presented an innovative, fresh analysis of Civil War soldiers. To be sure, Carmichael indicates that his book is not intended to be a rebuttal to the vast sea of literature on Civil War soldiers, but an effort to more thoroughly explore the lives of Union and Confederate soldiers. As his title suggests, however, Carmichael has waded into the waters of the "war for the common soldier." And in doing so, he has provided a more thorough, nuanced, and indeed pragmatic, understanding of Union and Confederate soldiers and the world in which they thought, fought, and survived.

Jennifer M. Murray is assistant professor of history at Oklahoma State University and the author of On a Great Battlefield: The Making, Management, and Memory of Gettysburg National Military Park *(2014).*

Union Command Failure in the Shenandoah: Major General Franz Sigel and the War in the Valley of Virginia, May 1864 by David A. Powell. El Dorado Hills, CA: Savas Beatie, 2019. ISBN: 978-1611214345.

Review by Eric Campbell

The Battle of New Market...suffers from no lack of drama, interest, or importance. The ramifications of the May 1864 engagement...were substantial. All three of the previous works are told largely from the Confederate point of view.... The dramatic part played by the Virginia Military Institute Cadets on that stormy May afternoon couldn't help but come to dominate the story.... But what of the Federals, and especially their commander, Franz Sigel? Sigel has been painted as more than a caricature than a commander. Almost every postwar account portrays Sigel as an obvious incompetent, and each of Sigel's decisions has been traditionally introduced as further proof of his battlefield negligence.... The rest of the Federal force...are reduced to little more than innocent victims of Sigel's blundering. David Powell's Union Command Failure in the Shenandoah Valley: Major General Franz Sigel and the War in the Valley of Virginia, May 1864, *provides the balance that has so long been needed. (xi)*

David Powell, well-known for his award winning trilogy on the Chickamauga Campaign, lays out the above challenge in his new book's introduction, and then proceeds to deliver on that challenge. *Union Command Failure in the Shenandoah: Major General Franz Sigel and the War in the Valley of Virginia, May 1864* is the first study of the 1864 spring campaign in the Shenandoah Valley from a Union perspective. The other three studies mentioned in the book's introduction above include Edmund Turner's *The New Market Campaign, May 1864* (Whittet & Shepperson: Richmond, 1912), William C. Davis' *The Battle of New Market* (Doubleday: New York, 1975) and Charles Knight's *Valley Thunder* (Savas Beatie: El Dorado Hill, California, 2010), and each concentrated its focus on the Southern perspective. True to his word, Powell (ironically a VMI graduate himself), examines the entire campaign from the Union point-of-view.

Broken down into nine chapters, the book does a masterful job of exploring the campaign from the strategic level (starting with how it fit into U.S. Grant's overall 1864 grand strategy, how Sigel was eventually chosen as the Union commander in the Shenandoah Valley, how the secondary campaign by Major General George Crook fit in, and how U.S. Grant's role in the planning of the campaign evolved, etc.), down to the tactical level of the regimental movements across the New Market battlefield.

The author's writing style is excellent, making it easy, even for the casual student of the Civil War, to follow the strategic and tactical movements and how they influenced each other. Eight excellent original maps by David Friedrichs accompany the text, also making it easier for the reader to understand the main flow of the narrative and the movements of the opposing armies. The book is also nicely illustrated, containing photographs of nearly all of the principal participants on both sides.

Powell's research is also very solid and, for the most part, well footnoted (which is absolutely essential for any book on an historical subject that wants to be taken seriously). The bibliography is quite lengthy for a study that runs slightly more than 200 pages. Powell packed a lot of information and analysis into a relatively short work. Nevertheless, it is well worth the read, and Powell more than proved his overall thesis:

> *Blaming everything on Franz Sigel strikes me as far too simple an explanation for what happened on the Federal side of the line during that rainy, thunderous afternoon. It is by no means my intention to seek to rehabilitate Sigel as the undiscovered military genius of the American Civil War. I do, however, think there is a great deal to be learned about why Sigel made the choices he did, and a close reading of history offers up valid reasons for many of those decisions. Sigel made significant mistakes, and those mistakes cost him the battle, but up to that point Sigel had also achieved much of what the Union higher command expected of him—a fact that goes largely unrecognized in the extant literature (pages xi-xii).*

Powell's *Union Command Failure in the Shenandoah Valley* now properly fills that gap.

Eric Campbell has worked as a ranger-historian for the National Park Service for thirty-four years, at a variety of sites, including twenty-four years at Gettysburg National Military Park. He has been the chief of interpretation at Cedar Creek and Belle Grove National Historical Park, which interprets all of the Civil War sites in the Shenandoah Valley, since 2009.

The Most Complete Political Machine Ever Known: The North's Union Leagues in the American Civil War by Paul Taylor. Kent, OH: Kent State University Press, 2018. ISBN: 978-1-60635-353-0.

Review by Kyle Rothemich

Loyalty to the Union during the Civil War has been central to our recent understandings of Union Civil War soldiers in the field. Paul Taylor's recent work *The Most Complete Political Machine Ever Known: The North's Union Leagues in the American Civil War* takes this framework and applies it to northern-noncombatants. Taylor argues that the antebellum culture of social clubs in wealthy northern social circles paved the way for the development of Union Leagues, whose main goal was to support the Union cause through written propaganda during the Civil War. Taylor highlights two supporting arguments early in his work: first, that Union Leagues were a "true grassroots movement," and second, the eventual reach of the Union Leagues nationalized northern definitions of loyalty and treason in the "court of public opinion." (12)

Union Leagues developed beginning in 1861 in Philadelphia, Boston, and New York to combat anti-Lincoln Democrats and Copperheads who League members saw as "treasonous" and a danger to the Union cause. The men who started these secret societies, such as Frederick Law Olmsted, were frequently wealthy and politically connected men who were sworn to secrecy through ritualistic initiation ceremonies. Initially Union Leagues did not affiliate with the Republican Party and simply wanted to boost the "Union" through writings and public oratories. However, as the Civil War entered its third and fourth years, Union Leagues were democratized in membership and became more explicitly pro-Republican in their messaging. Union Leagues and eventual Union Clubs sprouted outside of the wealthy eastern cities to the Midwest as their pro-Republican propaganda machine and message were nationalized. Taylor demonstrates that throughout the War, Union Leagues combatted Democrats' attempts to undermine Lincoln's war efforts and administration. This is most convincing in his account of the 1864 presidential election. Taylor recounts how Union Leagues strategically flooded the press with over six million pamphlets and articles arguing for Lincoln's re-election. "All these sources, taken as a whole, distributed over three pieces of pro-Republican or anti-Democrat propaganda for every single individual who voted for Lincoln in the 1864 election." (224)

Taylor's monograph spans twelve chapters and chronicles how Union Leagues launched a massive pro-Union public opinion campaign through pamphlets, broadsides, and newspaper articles. Taylor uses a plethora of primary sources including minutes from Union League meetings, published material from Union Leagues during the War, letters from members, and contemporary newspapers. Taylor suggests that the current historiography of Union Leagues, which frames them as a fringe political movement during the conflict and briefly during Reconstruction needs to be reconsidered. Taylor's examination of how Leagues used the court of public opinion to influence northern residents' conceptions of loyalty sheds new light onto the role of social clubs on the 19th century political landscape.

Readers of this journal should note Taylor's narrative of Union victories in the Shenandoah Valley in 1864 in connection with Union Leagues' efforts to re-elect Lincoln in November. The connection between battlefield victories and securing political support for Lincoln's second term is made stronger here than in other works that study the 1864 Shenandoah Valley Campaign. Taylor argues that Union Leagues' actions and efforts during Reconstruction to provide political support to freedmen also places Union Leagues on the same level as the Freedmen's Bureau. Readers will receive a fuller portrait of this transformative and all-consuming American era as Civil War scholarship continues to move from battlefield narratives and into the social and cultural realms of non-combatants. Union Leagues transformed how small groups of citizens can influence politics through the court of public opinion, and laid the groundwork for future political action groups.

Kyle Rothemich is a historian for the National Park Service at Cedar Creek and Belle Grove National Historical Park and manages the park's cultural resources program.

Illusions of Emancipation: The Pursuit of Freedom & Equality in the Twilight of Slavery by Joseph P. Reidy. Chapel Hill: University of North Carolina Press, 2019. ISBN: 978-1-4696-4836-1.

Review by Brian Matthew Jordan

Emancipation was a process that unfolded in contraband camps and in legislative chambers, on cotton plantations and in canebreaks, from the snake-choked bayous of Louisiana to the marshy sea islands of South Carolina. Synthesizing the tale of slavery's demise in the United States is thus an enormous challenge; a rich crop of recent scholarship has made it even more difficult. Building from the foundational work of the Freedmen and Southern Society Project, books by Chandra Manning, Amy Murrell Taylor, Jim Downs, and Glenn David Brasher—among others—have revealed anew the contingencies and complexities of the long struggle for black freedom in the nineteenth century.

Joseph P. Reidy attempts to make sense of emancipation with this book, the latest entry in the University of North Carolina's Littlefield History of the Civil War Era series. His hefty tome, informed by decades of reading and original research, caps a distinguished career spent studying the halting and contingent manner in which slavery was uprooted in the United States.

Reidy divides his study into three parts. Each considers one of the "frameworks" through which "members of the Civil War generation attempted both to understand and to help chart a way through the extraordinary events that swirled around them daily." (16) The first framework is "time." Rejecting the once commonplace notion that emancipation unfolded in a "linear" way, the author restores to view the "repeated setbacks—often accompanied by self-doubt" that characterized the destruction of slavery. (44) Seasons, he points out, not only helped to define one's "chances of becoming free," but "also figured metaphorically into emancipation." (59) Americans wrestled with the meaning of the "revolutionary forces" unbridled by war, but were nonetheless cognizant, as was Colonel Thomas Wentworth Higginson, that "revolutions may go backward." (107)

If time was "elastic," so too was "space," which supplies Reidy's second framework. (126) Not surprisingly, many freedom-seeking slaves came to associate freedom with the presence of Union soldiers. Still, "combatants and civilians alike experienced the whipsaw effects of safe space rendered dangerous and vice versa," especially in areas like the Shenandoah Valley. (127) War uprooted families, ruined plantations, and created refugees who crowded into often unhygienic contraband camps. Emancipation also unfolded differently in different spaces, mocking the "progressive narrative" popular a generation ago. (171)

"Home" is the third framework. Emancipation broached debates about the place of newly-freed slaves in the reborn nation. "The Civil War," Reidy writes, "was about citizenship as much as it was about slavery." (231) White Northerners fretted about a potential wave of African-American migration, while free blacks seized the moment to militate against racial segregation. (319-320) Finally, despite their "best efforts," the "Radical Republicans of the Civil War era failed to guarantee basic citizenship rights for the freed people, much less to address the structural economic and social conditions that reproduced oppression and poverty." (355)

Taken together, these frameworks restore to view the raw, lived immediacy of emancipation. The Civil War, like emancipation, did not always move in logical, rational, or easy to apprehend ways. Peering through three prisms familiar to Civil War Americans, Reidy's book demonstrates the constant reckoning that the conflict demanded of the enslaved (who, of course, did not know how the war would turn out). The book's tripartite structure results in some repetition of themes and ideas, but this hardly detracts from its accomplishments. Here is emancipation as it unfolded on the ground—wobbly and faltering, subject to setbacks, surprises, and misfortunes. Reidy's emancipation is ultimately darker, messier, and more restless than many previous historians have described. Still, through it all, he finds "hope" in our "illusions of emancipation." (356)

Brian Matthew Jordan is assistant professor of history Sam Houston State University. His book Marching Home: Union Veterans and Their Unending Civil War (2014) was a finalist for the Pulitzer Prize.

The 30th North Carolina Infantry in the Civil War by William Thomas Venner. Jefferson, NC: McFarland & Co., 2018. ISBN: 978-1476-662404.

Review by Jeff Felton

Though social history has dominated the field of Civil War studies in recent decades, military histories of the war continue to provide fruitful, accessible, and useful research into what may seem an overcrowded field. One feature of Civil War military history that remains popular is unit histories (company, regiment, or brigade), such as William Thomas Venner's *The 30th North Carolina Infantry in the Civil War: A History and Roster*. This new addition to the field provides an excellent account of a Confederate combat infantry regiment that focuses on the words of the men to describe their history.

Histories of North Carolina units are abundant dating back as far as 1901. Venner's study of the 30th North Carolina is an excellent companion to Michael W. Taylor's *To Drive the Enemy from Southern Soil: The Letters of Col. Francis Marion Parker and the*

History of the 30th Regiment North Carolina Troops. Taylor's work not only published the letters of the regiment's commander, Francis Parker, but used the letters as a backdrop to tell the story of the regiment. *The 30th North Carolina Infantry in the Civil War* is a more thorough history of the regiment and complements Taylor's work very well by providing a history of the regiment as told through the eyes of the soldiers. Though Venner uses many of the same sources that Taylor did, it should not detract from his contribution with this volume.

Chronologically organized, Venner takes the reader through the experience of a veteran regiment of North Carolinians in the Confederate Army of Northern Virginia from their organization to the surrender at Appomattox Court House. The most useful contribution of the book is an exhaustive set of appendices that lists the names of the men who served in the regiment with useful personal information on each soldier. Another useful addition to this roster is Venner's inclusion of data of men who joined the regiment after 1861 or were conscripted after April 1862. In addition to the roster is a comprehensive listing of casualties throughout the war. Venner listed the names of each casualty, the battle or skirmish, company within the regiment, and what happened to the individual. Similar lists are found throughout the text as Venner lists the total number of casualties within each company and the regiment as a whole. This should provide useful information for researchers as well as genealogists looking to find what a family member went through during the war as well as his participation in it. In addition to the inter-chapter casualty figures are lists of the number of men present at the start of a particular campaign or battle. By including these lists, Venner shows the reader the costs of a particular battle on a single regiment. Photographs of soldiers are included throughout the text as well as maps showing the location and movements of the regiment.

The 30th North Carolina Infantry was typical of many Civil War regiments in that its members left behind hundreds of letters, diaries, and recollections detailing their service. The regiment was one of four regiments in Brigadier General Stephen Dodson Ramseur's North Carolina Brigade. The 30th participated in every action of the Army of Northern Virginia from June 1862 until the army surrendered in April 1865.

One of this book's strengths is the use of a copious number

of letters and memoirs to tell the story of the 30th North Carolina. Venner's use of the primary sources conveys a sense of immediacy to the daily life of veteran combat troops in the Civil War. Venner uses over 2,000 quotes, which allows readers to experience the world the soldiers lived, fought, and died in. Venner, in addition to the narrative, provides a comprehensive roster, casualty study, and data detailing how many men of the regiment were present at the beginning and end of a particular battle. This material was taken from census data and service records.

More analysis of personnel, decisions, and motivations would have strengthened the book. For instance, what effect did defeats have on the morale of the men of the regiment? How did these men react to secession, slavery, Lincoln, conscription and other topics? What were the men's initial and sustaining motivations throughout the war? These questions and more deserved to be answered in order to gain a fuller understanding of Civil War units. Utilizing frameworks such as environmental history and new military history could offer a fresh view of the average Confederate soldier, and this type of unit history should be pursued in order to steer the niche away from strictly narrative recitations and embrace a more personal and varied story. Venner's history of the 30th is a straightforward narrative history of a veteran Confederate regiment serving in the Confederacy's main army and an excellent addition to any Civil War or North Carolina history library.

Jeff Felton is a resource protection associate for the Shenandoah Valley Battlefields Foundation in New Market, Virginia. He received his BA in history from Bridgewater College and his MA in history from Virginia Tech. He is the author of an essay in Volume II of the Journal of the Shenandoah Valley During the Civil War Era *and is currently working on a history of Stephen D. Ramseur's North Carolina Brigade.*

The Most Desperate Acts of Gallantry: George A. Custer in the Civil War by Daniel T. Davis. El Dorado Hills, CA: Savas Beatie, 2019. ISBN: 978-1611214116.

Review by Jonathan M. Steplyk

George Armstrong Custer seems frozen in American history,

circled by his dwindling 7th Cavalry troopers on Last Stand Hill, surrounded by fierce Plains warriors. Yet Custer first rose to national prominence during the Civil War, achieving a meteoric rise that established him as one of the most aggressive and formidable cavalrymen on either side. In *The Most Desperate Acts of Gallantry*, historian Daniel T. Davis offers a fast-paced study of Custer's Civil War career as part of the Emerging Civil War series.

Custer graduated from West Point in 1861, just in time for the opening campaigns in Virginia. His career as a junior officer reads much like a dime store novel, participating in cavalry charges, reconnaissance missions, and a balloon ascent, as well as serving on the staffs of several key generals. Shortly after Brandy Station, Custer received the promotion that vaulted him up ranks to the command of a brigade in Alfred Pleasanton's newly-constituted Cavalry Corps. The "Boy General" and his Michigan troopers skirmished with J. E. B. Stuart's cavalry in the opening stages of the Gettysburg Campaign. Custer clashed again with Rebel troopers at the battle itself, personally leading charges that helped blunt Stuart's July 3 maneuvers. The Confederate retreat into Virginia saw Custer and his Wolverines in still more action as Union cavalry hounded Rebel rearguards.

The conflict's final year brought new laurels to Custer as Philip Sheridan reinvented the Army of the Potomac's cavalry as a combat arm that could meet Confederate cavalry on their own terms. His Wolverines grappled with the Rebels at Yellow Tavern, where a pistol shot from one of Custer's men slew Stuart himself. At Trevilian Station, Custer pounced on a Confederate supply train in what turned out to be a gap between two enemy cavalry divisions. The surrounded Michigan Brigade found itself desperately fighting off attacks on three fronts, holding out until relieved by the arrival of Wesley Merritt's brigade. Both Custer and Merritt followed their chief Phil Sheridan to the Shenandoah Valley. There Custer and his shock tactics contributed to Union victories at Third Winchester, Tom's Brook, and Cedar Creek, engagements that often pitted Custer against his old West Point roommate Tom Rosser. Custer closed his Civil War career once again in Sheridan's Cavalry Corps, helping break Confederate forces at Five Forks and trap Lee's army at Appomattox.

Davis successfully chronicles Custer's better-known engagements such as Gettysburg and Tom's Brook, but also lesser known actions such as his service in the post-Gettysburg pursuit of Lee's army and the winter phase of the 1864 Valley Campaign. From the narrative a clear picture emerges of Custer's talents as a combat commander. Custer, he observes, often relied on attacks calculated to strike the enemy on the front and on a flank, a tactic that often tipped battles in his favor. Davis also points out that Custer's flashiness and lead-from-the-front style of command did not reflect arrogance or recklessness, as many then and now have assumed, but were rather keys to his success as a cavalry leader: "Custer recognized that if an officer distinguished himself to those he led, terror quite often turned into inspiration, a key element to success or survival on the battlefield." (122)

Davis does not offer an uncritical hagiography of Custer, however. He challenges "the popular image of Custer...single-handedly fending off Jeb Stuart's Confederates" at Gettysburg, arguing that credit is also due Brigadier General David Gregg, under whose authority Custer served that day. Davis also highlights the contribution to the Michigan Brigade's exploits of Battery M, 2nd U.S. Artillery, ably commanded by Alexander Pennington, who by the time of Cedar Creek was leading one of Custer's brigades. Perhaps most fascinating are the parallels the author draws between Custer's Civil War service and his defeat at the Little Bighorn. Once again, Custer had planned converging attacks on the enemy. When those initial attacks failed, Custer's command once again found itself in desperate straits, hoping for timely reinforcements. But unlike Trevilian Station, no relief arrived on that fateful June day in 1876.

The Most Desperate Acts of Gallantry is an engaging study of Custer's Civil War service. Davis writes feelingly about his subject, bookending the work with vignettes of a visit to the Little Bighorn battlefield. In keeping with the Emerging Civil War series, the book is richly illustrated, complemented by an appendix of essays covering Custer's distinguished brother Tom, his beloved wife Libbie, his historical memory, and assessment of his generalship. Together these make for a memorable and worthwhile exploration of one of the Civil War's most colorful generals.

Jonathan M. Steplyk is the author of Fighting Means Killing: Civil War Soldiers and the Nature of Combat. *He is an adjunct assistant professor of History at the University of Texas at Arlington and formerly worked as a seasonal ranger at Cedar*

Creek and Belle Grove National Historical Park.

The 96th Pennsylvania Volunteers in the Civil War by David A. Ward. Jefferson, NC: McFarland & Co., 2018. ISBN: 978-1476-668512.

Review by Kevin Pawlak

Regimental histories are one of the original narratives in the field of Civil War history. First written and published by veterans, the task of completing such works has now fallen to historians. David A. Ward's study of the 96th Pennsylvania Infantry is the latest entry into this category of the Civil War's historiography.

Ward set out to produce the first narrative history of the 96th Pennsylvania's service, a task, he acknowledges, that several of the veterans were fit to do themselves, but never did. This book seeks to "broaden our understanding of the common soldier of the Civil War and add to our sum knowledge" of the conflict. (5)

The 96th Pennsylvania Infantry was raised in the coal region of eastern Pennsylvania's Schuylkill County. Like all Civil War regiments, its ranks represented the community from which it derived. Native-born Pennsylvanians comprised most of the regiment though a growing immigrant population in the county represented roughly one-quarter of the unit's soldiers. Not surprisingly, the coal mines drew most of the immigrants to the region.

This ethnically mixed group of men learned to become soldiers. They endured the rigors of military drill, discipline, and life in the army. Ward traces the raising of the regiment and its early embodiment as soldiers of Lincoln's army. But while his narrative predominantly follows the regiment through the war's eastern theater, Ward does not lose sight of how the soldiers' upbringing and homes influenced their wartime experiences. Likewise, he continually ties the soldiers on the battlefield to the civilians they left behind on the home front, showing that the two were in a symbiotic relationship. "We had better lose a battle in the field than that you lose the contest at home," said one regimental officer in the local *Miners' Journal* newspaper. (195) The author's mining of a vast array of primary sources demonstrates that connection, particularly in sections where soldiers wrote home to their family and friends expressing the importance of local, state, and national politics to their efforts on the front lines.

Any regimental history of a unit as involved in multiple large battles of the Civil War must trace the regiment's action throughout the war. Ward's book excels here. His battle descriptions mix together the larger picture of the campaign, the situation on the battlefield for the men of the 96th Pennsylvania, and human-interest stories to keep the narrative flowing. By exploring in detail the role that this regiment played in battles such as Gaines' Mill, Crampton's Gap, and Spotsylvania Courthouse, among others, readers who have a particular interest in those battles are likely to find something new. The 96th Pennsylvania Infantry also experienced the evolution of battlefield tactics during its term, from a stand-up firefight at Crampton's Gap to a bayonet charge under Emory Upton at Spotsylvania. This aspect of their service is explored and fits the story of this one regiment into the larger narrative of the Civil War.

For as much change as the 96th Pennsylvania helped usher in on numerous battlefields, their participation in combat equally shaped them. The men of the regiment came to realize through their service the need for changing war aims and a harder war against the Confederacy as long as it would actually bring the conflict to a speedier conclusion.

Ward's grasp of numerous primary sources related to the regiment aids him in painting a very complete picture of the regiment. Additionally, many images of soldiers discussed in the text abound through the book's pages. Excellent maps equally help piece together the book's battle narratives.

Some authors of regimental histories tend to overreach in their conclusions about their subject's contributions to their respective war effort. Ward narrowly skirts around this trap and claims through their heroism on many battlefields, "the regiment contributed significantly to eventual Union victory." (276)

A regimental history of the 96th Pennsylvania Infantry has been wanting for a long time. This book has made the wait worth it. It provides an in-depth look at one small facet of the Civil War but it never loses sight of the context in which the 96th Pennsylvania fought the war. Ward's welcome volume makes it a standard-bearer for other authors seeking to write regimental histories to follow.

Kevin Pawlak is a historic site manager for the Prince William County Historic

Preservation Division and the author of three books about the Civil War.

Valley Thunder: The Battle of New Market and the Opening of the Shenandoah Valley Campaign, May 1864 by Charles R. Knight. El Dorado Hills, CA: 2018. ISBN: 978-1611214222.

Review by Brandon H. Beck

1864 was the last full year of the War, and by any measure the most trying, North and South. Serious fighting began in February, while in the autumn, voters in the Union would decide whether or not to retain Abraham Lincoln in office. For Lincoln to be reelected, the war for the Union would have to go well.

The Union had won the strategic initiative in 1863. U.S. Grant, Lincoln's new general-in-chief, now proposed a strategy that would put heavy and relentless pressure on what remained of the Confederacy. Union forces, large and small, would advance in Florida, Mississippi, Alabama, Georgia, and Virginia. The Confederates would be unable to move forces from one front to another, as in September 1863. Viewed from Washington, the larger Union forces seemed to be in safe hands—Grant, with Meade, with the Army of the Potomac, and Sherman, commanding the conglomerate of armies aiming for Atlanta. With the smaller forces, however, there were many questions. General Truman Seymour, defeated at Olustee in Florida on February 20, and General William S. Smith, defeated two days later at Okolona, Mississippi, may not have been "political generals" in an election year, but they were incompetent. But in May, three generals taking the field were certainly appointed for their political constituencies rather than their military competence.

First off the mark was General Benjamin Butler, aiming for Petersburg in the Bermuda Hundred Campaign (May 6-22) but bottled up on the small peninsula. Then, from May 18-22, General Nathaniel Banks, whose target was to have been Mobile, was stopped along the Red River in Louisiana. Finally, General Franz Sigel, assigned to the Shenandoah Valley, was defeated and driven back in the Battle of New Market on May 15. Of these three Confederate successes (Olustee, Okolona, and New Market), New Market is the best known, largely because of the gallant charge of the Virginia Military Institute's cadets.

Between 1975 and 2000 the definitive book about New Market was William C. Davis' still excellent *The Battle of New Market*. But Charles Knight's *Valley Thunder* supersedes the older. Davis himself is glad to acknowledge Knight's achievement. In Knight's forward, Davis writes that "Valley Thunder is simply the last word we are ever likely to have or need on this crucial small action in 1864." (ix)

Following Davis, Knight never loses sight of the big picture, or wider context. He sets forth the logistical and strategic importance of the Valley, as well as the largely Confederate sympathies of its population. As May approached, the author explains how Sigel intended to employ the strategic initiative. Staunton was the objective, as the meeting place of three Union commands: General George Crook, with 6,000 men, coming by way of Dublin and Blacksburg, General William Averell, with 7,000, by way of Saltville, and Sigel's own command, approximately 9,000 men, coming up the Valley Pike from Winchester. Once united the force might cross the Blue Ridge, or continue on to Lynchburg. (Grant believed that cutting the railroad there was the most important objective). However, as Knight explains, neither Crook nor Averell reached Staunton. Sigel was left alone in what Knight calls the "Valley of Defeat." With Crook and Averell in retreat, Confederate general John C. Breckinridge could now focus on Sigel.

At Staunton, Breckinridge concentrated about 4,000 men, including General John C. Imboden's cavalry and 257 Cadets from the Virginia Military Institute.

As Sigel came south from Winchester, he became more and more vulnerable. Imboden and John Mosby, making a rare appearance in a major operation, harassed the Federals without let up. Sigel detached two columns in in vain pursuit of his tormentors. Both met defeat, which Knight explains in detail. As his strength diminished, Sigel's march became disjointed. Knight's maps make clear to the reader what Imboden urged on his chief— rather than stand at Staunton, Breckinridge should come fast down the Valley and meet the Federals head on.

Regarding the march south, I was somewhat confused on pages 97-99 about Breckinridge's departure on May 13 and the distances covered in his marches. What is clear is that although Imboden could not hold New Market against Sigel's advance, he and Breckinridge joined forces on May 14, to carry the fight to Sigel the next day.

The battle of New Market was a hard fight. Sigel may or may not have shouted orders in his native German, but Breckinridge kept the initiative throughout the day. On the field he accompanied the guns in person. Rather than remain in a static position Breckinridge decided it would be more effective if the artillery leap frogged ahead of the infantry.

Knight describes the fighting in just enough detail to keep the narrative moving to its great conclusion—the charge of the cadets. Sigel's command had resisted hard all day, and the cadets' charge was a last and reluctant resort.

There is a full and current bibliography, and eight interesting appendices. One discusses what is perhaps the battle's next most well-known story, that of the shell struck post near St. Mathew's Church.

The Confederacy took heart from the small successes of early 1864. It deserved to. But although Sherman and Grant could be checked, and slowed, they could not be stopped. Even in the Valley a new Union thrust soon followed Sigel's defeat. Knight aptly notes that by the first week of June the outcome of the New Market fight was immaterial.

Brandon H. Beck, PhD is professor emeritus of history at Shenandoah University and the founding director of the University's McCormick Civil War Institute. He is the author of numerous books on Civil War history.

Notes on Contributors

Donna Dodenhoff has enjoyed a long career in public history. She received her PhD in American Studies from the College of William & Mary in 2016 and continues her research on the pending crisis of the Union in the 1840's and '50's and the Reconstruction era.

Jake Gabriele graduated from Shenandoah University in 2018 with a BS in history and is currently enrolled in the PhD program in history at Mississippi State University. In the summer of 2018 Jake was one of the McCormick Civil War Institute's Miles' Summer Fellows.

Robert Grandchamp is the award winning author of fifteen books on American military history, including *The Boys of Adams' Battery G, The Seventh Rhode Island Infantry, Rhody Redlegs*, and most recently *Rhode Island's Civil War Dead: A Complete Roster*. Robert earned his MA in American History from Rhode Island College. He is a former National Park Service Ranger with service at Harpers Ferry, Shenandoah, and Blackstone Valley. He is currently a senior analyst with the federal government and resides in Jericho Center, Vermont, with his wife Elizabeth and their children.

Jon-Erik Gilot, a native of Mount Pleasant, Ohio, is a graduate of Bethany College, where he received a BA in History, and Kent State University, where he received an MLIS with a concentration in archival studies. He has contributed to several books and numerous publications and is a contributing author at Emerging Civil War. He is employed as Director of Archives & Records at the Diocese of Wheeling-Charleston in Wheeling, West Virginia.

Victor Herrera is an English and history major at Shenandoah University. During the summer of 2018 Victor was one of the McCormick Civil War Institute's Miles' Summer Fellows.

Jonathan A. Noyalas is director of Shenandoah University's McCormick Civil War Institute and founding editor of the *Journal of the Shenandoah Valley During the Civil War Era*. He is the author or editor of twelve books on Civil War era history and has contributed more than 100 articles, essays, reviews, and book chapters to a variety of scholarly and popular publications including *Civil War History, Civil War Times, Civil War Monitor,* and *America's Civil War*. He is the recipient of numerous awards for his teaching, scholarship, and service including the highest honor that can be bestowed upon a professor at a college/university in the Old Dominion—the State Council for Higher Education in Virginia's Outstanding Faculty Award.

Sarah Powell graduated from Shenandoah University in May 2019 with a BS in history and a recipient of Shenandoah's Bartley History Award. She is a volunteer with the McCormick Civil War Institute at Shenandoah University's Cool Spring

Battlefield campus.

Trish Ridgeway served as director of the Handley Regional Library from 1993 to 2013. She holds a MS in Library Science from Florida State University, an MA in English from Winthrop College, and a BS from Radford College. In 2001, with her husband Harry (and several others), she helped found the Old Court House Civil War Museum, now known as the Shenandoah Valley Civil War Museum. She served on the board of the museum until the Shenandoah Valley Battlefields Foundation took over the reins of the museum in 2016. Currently, Trish is writing a book about Judge Richard Parker.

Shelby R. Shrader graduated from Shenandoah University in May 2017 with a BS in history. She was the first recipient of the McCormick Civil War Institute's Miles' Summer Fellowship. She reviews regularly for *Civil War News* and serves on the McCormick Civil War Institute's advisory board.

Prue Engle Yelinek is an ordained minister (retired) in the Church of the Brethren. As a great-great-granddaughter of Sheridan refugees John and Rebecca Wine Bowman, she enjoys researching her family's deep roots in the Shenandoah Valley and their interface with Church of the Brethren history and Civil War studies. She and her husband, Ed, who serves as chief research assistant, live in Greencastle, Pennsylvania.

Made in the
USA
Middletown, DE

76720445R00092